David Bowie Biography
The Rebel, Icon, and Shape-Shifter of Rock

James Raymon Gunn

"I don't know where I'm going from here, but I promise it won't be boring."

CONTENTS

Part One: I'm hoping I can make it on my own.
Chapter 1: When I'm Five Years Old
Chapter 2: Considering Me
Chapter 3: Every Madman

Part Two: Things That Are Hollow
Chapter 4: It is not free to change.
Chapter 5: Make me cry and break down
Chapter 6: I Am Not a Weirdo
Chapter 7: Fuck off, it's my life.
Chapter 8: The Filthy Lesson of the Heart
Chapter 9: Houdini's Mechanism

Part One:
I'm hoping I can make it on my own.

Chapter 1: When I'm Five Years Old

David Bowie instructed his chauffeur to take the leisurely road to the Brixton Academy on a chilly, wet November in 1991, just like the cold, wet Novembers of his childhood. The smoke-filled bus slowed down Stansfield Road, just a few hundred yards from the event, and paused outside a huge, inconspicuous three-story Victorian mansion before continuing on its way.

In the previous twelve weeks, Bowie had been gregarious, honest, and almost startlingly vulnerable, but he stayed silent for a few minutes while he glanced out the window. When he looked back, guitarist Eric Schermerhorn, who was sitting next to him, noticed tears streaming down his boss's face. 'It's a miracle,' Bowie said quietly. He was unafraid of showing his vulnerabilities. 'I should have been an accountant,' I think. I'm not sure how this happened.'

For Schermerhorn, who had witnessed Bowie's flair and grace up close, the thought of David Robert Jones scrutinizing a company spreadsheet was absurd. He didn't even know if he could sing, as he'd indicated to Schermerhorn a few days previously. This apparent self-doubt was strange to Schermerhorn, who had witnessed the man's nearly supernatural ability to hold a show together and dominate a crowd. Over the next few months, Schermerhorn would learn about Bowie's organization, his "executive abilities," and his talent for working the system via Bowie's pals and his own observations. Yet here was the guy himself, observing the scene of his youth, convinced that it was all a mistake. The concept appeared absurd. Wasn't someone this beautiful always destined to be a star?

David Bowie has referred to himself as a 'Brixton boy' several times. Despite the fact that his stay was brief, it is an appropriate description. Brixton in January 1947 was a one-of-a-kind location: the cultural heart of south London, endowed with its own racy glitz, beaten but unbowed by the Luftwaffe and Hitler's terror weapons, the devastation of which could be seen wherever you walked.

When World War II broke out, Haywood was among the first to enlist, joining the Royal Fusiliers and fighting in France, North Africa, and Europe. Haywood rejoined Barnardo's as General Superintendent to the Chief of Staff when he returned to a devastated but victorious London in October 1945. Haywood's marriage, like many others during the war, ended in divorce, most likely due to an affair with a nurse that resulted in a child, Annette, born in 1941.

Brixton was cold, damp, soot-blackened, and pummeled by vengeance weapons in the immediate post-war years. Brixton's pre-war raciness and music-hall glamor were further heightened by its recent history, and in 1947 Brixton appeared exceptionally dystopian, to borrow one of David's favorite terms. During WWII, Churchill's spymasters distorted press reports of where Hitler's futuristic V1 flying bombs were landing, ensuring they fell short and hit south London rather than the rich West End. Over forty pioneering cruise missiles blasted into Brixton and Lambeth, flattening entire streets both behind and in front of the Jones' family home. The majority of the rubble had been removed by 1947, but the region remained its menacing gap-toothed appearance for decades.

David's first winter was miserable. Britain in late 1947 was in a bad way. The Second World War energized the American economy, but it left Britain exhausted, damaged, and on the verge of bankruptcy. There were no street lights, no coal, gas supplies were low, and ration cards were still required to purchase linen, gasoline, 'economy' clothes, eggs, and the scraggy scraps of Argentine beef that were only available on rare occasions. Christopher Isherwood, the novelist who would later encourage David to relocate to Berlin, visited London that year and was astounded by its squalor. 'London is fading,' a resident warned him, encouraging him not to return.

Life was difficult for parents. The abandoned, bomb-damaged houses were playgrounds and museums, full of exciting items abandoned by long-vanished residents, for the children who scampered through this urban wilderness.

David adored his father, and he still wears a gold cross given to him by Haywood when he was in his teens, but when asked about his relationship with his mother in 2002, he recalled Philip Larkin's famously grim 'This Be The Verse', which begins, 'They fuck you up, your mum and dad.' The occasion was an informal live discussion with interviewer Michael Parkinson; the lines, like many of David's remarks, elicited laughter. The titters turned to uncomfortable stillness as David continued to recite the final words of anguish.

The Madness' of Peggy Burns' family would become part of the Bowie legend, but for the young David Jones, it was distance - a fundamental absence of emotion - that defined his relationship with his mother. Peggy's sister Pat described their mother, Margaret Mary Burns, née Heaton, as a "cold woman." There wasn't much love in the air.' Peggy seemed to have inherited her mother's coldness. According to family legend, Peggy worked as a nanny in her childhood before falling in love with the gorgeous Jack Isaac Rosenberg, son of a wealthy Jewish furrier. Rosenberg vowed to marry Peggy, but vanished before the birth of their son, Terence Guy Adair Burns, on November 5, 1937.

Peggy's past held darker shadows as well. In 1986, her sister Pat - dubbed 'the terrible aunt' by Bowie - went on the record to discuss the Burns family's tumultuous history. Peggy and Pat's siblings included three sisters, Nora, Una, and Vivienne, who, according to Pat, suffered from various degrees of mental instability; what one journalist referred to as the Burns' "family affliction." This background later inspired the belief that David Jones was obliged to create alter-egos in order to escape the craziness within. Ken Pitt, David's future manager, knew David, Peggy, and Pat better than anybody else and finds this hypothesis "unconvincing." Although David would later gleefully celebrate his family, declaring,'most of them are nutty - in, just out of, or about to enter an institution,' most people who knew them found Haywood friendly and sincere, and Peggy talkative once you got to know her, with many traces of her former vivaciousness.

As David grew into a toddler, austerity remained tight, but rays of hope began to show. 1953, a year many children remember fondly, saw the end of sweet rationing and the introduction of television. Haywood Jones was one of hundreds who purchased a new television set in order to watch the coronation of the gorgeous young Queen Elizabeth. Only a few weeks later, the six-year-old David crept downstairs to see The Quatermass Experiment, a groundbreaking BBC science-fiction series that had the entire country enthralled to the television. This 'terrific series' would leave an impression on David, who recalls watching it every Saturday night "from behind the sofa when my parents thought I had gone to bed." 'After each show, I would sneak back to my bedroom, stiff with anxiety, because the action seemed so forceful.' The show triggered a lifelong interest in science fiction and - through its theme tune, the dark, terrifying Mars, The Bringer of War from Holst's 'Planet Suite' - the emotional power of music.

David's residence at 40 Stansfield Road was a spacious three-story terraced Victorian property shared with two other families for the majority of their eight years in Brixton. David Bowie later portrayed his Brixton boyhood as a "walk on the wild side," with gangs roving the streets, with a traditional rock-star twist. The neighborhood kids did indeed roam freely, but their prey consisted of butterflies, tadpoles, and other urban animals. 'It was unbelievable,' says David's next-door neighbor and schoolmate Sue Larner, 'there were these big areas from the bomb sites, and collapsed buildings, which appeared like mountains to us, covered in buddleia: these were our playgrounds.' The derelict buildings at the bottom of Stansfield Road were sinister, yet fragrant - kids scurried around the sweet-smelling blooms with nets, because there were more butterflies than ever before or since, and the many pools and ponds in south London's abandoned bomb sites were teeming with tadpoles and newts. Rats also casually sauntered about the abandoned buildings, and local children recall mice running through the drafty, uncarpeted Victorian houses at night, clutching a hot water bottle for warmth and comfort.

The Jones family remained to themselves in those early years. Most local children played on the streets, but David mostly stayed with his mother, and Haywood spent his days at Barnardo's in Stepney. David began school at Stockwell Infants, a three-minute walk from his home on Stockwell Road, one of Brixton's principal thoroughfares, in 1951. He recalls peeing his pants on the first day; fortunately, Bertha Douglas, the nice milk lady, kept a supply of clean panties on hand for such ordinary eventualities. The high Victorian edifice of Stockwell Infants appeared austere, with its characteristic odor of disinfection and rubber plimsolls, but the staff was largely caring and compassionate. 'It was a sweet, friendly school; small and intimate,' recalls Suzanne Liritis, a classmate. 'The professors used to tell us things like, "you're special, Jesus loves you," recalls Sue Larner, her friend.

Most of the households on Stansfield Road were large, with children accompanied by siblings and sisters on their trips. Perhaps this is why so few of them remember David. Sue Larner was one of the few kids who noticed him; now a sculptor, she recalls noting the nice-looking, well-groomed boy's artistic talent. 'Neither of us had much experience with boys, but I recall giving him a few techniques on the drawing board - and he showed me many more. He demonstrated how to draw a woman's bonnet with the neck without first drawing a face. He was excellent.'

David's universe was bounded by the bomb sites on Chantrey Road and the far side of Stockwell Road, where all kids played: turning left on Stockwell Road, he'd immediately reach the school playground; turning right, he'd walk past two sweet shops, the nearest overseen by a kindly, camp gentleman. Further down Stockwell Road was the Astoria: subsequently renamed the Academy and home to David Bowie, it was nevertheless a flourishing local theater in the 1950s, with morning matinees showcasing cowboy pictures, Zorro, or Laurel and Hardy. A bookshop extended out onto the pavement on the approach to the cinema, loaded with comics and children's books. The principal feature that dominated Stockwell Road was Pride and Clarke's, a famed motorbike and vehicle showroom that extended across a series of maroon-painted buildings and was later immortalized in Antonioni's Blowup. This was where David, the future petrolhead, could admire BSAs, Rileys, and other iconic British motorcycles and automobiles.

The acclaimed poet laureate, John Betjeman, identified the suburbs as the home of a "new kind of citizen." David's new home, Bromley, was also the birthplace of H. G. Wells, a fitting testament to its futurism.

David started at Burnt Ash School a few years after the majority of his classmates and didn't stand out much throughout the first few terms. Within a year or two, David had become a member of a small gang that included Dudley Chapman and John Barrance, who lived nearby and were invited to David's eighth birthday celebration. Many children, even at this age, noticed the confined inside of the Jones' small two-up, two-down house. John Barrance observed that the family seemed reserved and quiet. 'They were quite friendly, but I suppose they had a "don't touch this, don't touch that" approach,' says the author. Max Batten, David's companion, spent more relaxed moments with him, eating lollipops, conversing with Mrs Jones, and slipping upstairs and unwrapping Haywood's service revolver one unforgettable afternoon. The two boys toyed with it secretly before gently placing it back in the drawer where it had been hidden.

Though few of his contemporaries recall it as anything out of the norm, David's upbringing would subsequently be depicted as dysfunctional - largely by David himself. When he was in his most flamboyantly insane phase, in the mid-1970s, he used to say, "Everyone finds empathy in a nutty family." Peggy in particular was singled out as the ideal embodiment of repression and eccentricity, but the most damning recollection of others is that she was a snob. In general, only the more middle-class youngsters were greeted with a smile and a cup of tea at Plaistow Grove, and David seemed to figure out which of his friends deserved to be ushered in the front door and which deserved to wait at the garden gate. To be honest, it's likely Peggy simply favored boys who, like David, had been taught to say "please" and "thank you." John Hutchinson, a well-bred Yorkshire guy who enjoyed sitting in the rear room with its pleasant fireplace and portraits on the mantelpiece, recalls that she was nice, recalling how she would knit costumes for his baby son, Christian, in later years. Some of the problems between Peggy and David were simply due to the generational shift that would soon sweep the country, the arrival of the adolescent, and the fact that, as Hutchinson puts it, "it became cool to put down your parents." Other familial tensions were witnessed by Peggy's sister Pat in later years. Terry was supposedly left behind in Brixton during their first year in Bromley because it was deemed to be more convenient for his employment as a clerk in Southwark. Later, he rejoined David, Peggy, and Haywood at Plaistow Grove, but his visit was brief; none of David's friends recall seeing him at the Jones' house before he went to prepare for National Service in 1955. If parents 'screw you up,' as David phrased it, Terry suffered far more than his brother.

One kid described Headmaster George Lloyd as "interesting." He took music and literature sessions, coaching his students one-on-one. He was slightly portly and jovial. He was 'kind,' loving with the children, and frequently sat with boys as they read, putting his arm around the preferred student. There were a few boys for whom he seemed to have genuine feelings, 'and one of them was David,' says a classmate. He clearly admired David.'

David, who was ten or eleven years old, had delicate, almost elfin features, bangs on his hair, was ordinary height, and slightly slender. But he had an intensity and enthusiasm about him that seemed to win over George Lloyd and others, the beginnings of a talent for charm. He was a good-looking boy, which his female peers recognized later, and by his twenties he was acquiring a skill for using charm "as a weapon," according to a later confidante, writer Charles Shaar Murray. 'Even if you'd had a falling out, you'd be convinced within five minutes of meeting David again that he'd hardly been able to function in the years he hadn't seen you. I admit that I had a platonic crush on him for a while.'

It was this charm, this ability to be whoever his confidante wanted him to be, that would shape David Bowie; it was what got him his breaks, the opportunity his ever-active intellect figured out how to take advantage of. That appeal was not used as intensively or as mercilessly in the early days. 'He was just, somehow, one of the kids you noticed,' remembers classmate Jan Powling, 'intelligent, fairly hilarious, with gobs of personality.' He was always more well dressed than his classmates: 'always well scrubbed, with clean fingernails,' adds Powling. 'In a nutshell, he's the kind of boy you'd be proud of if you were his mother.'

David Jones, eleven, was well-groomed, courteous, and every suburban mother's dream son. He also followed middle-class customs by joining the local Scout Pack and Church of England choir. 'We were flung in,' recounts fellow cub scout Geoff MacCormack, 'because that's what parents used to do with their kids back then. We didn't make a fuss about it; we just went on with it.' The youth, like Keith Richards, one of Baden-Powell's most unlikely fans, relished the outdoor experiences. The weekly pack meetings and services became an important part of David's life because it was there that he met MacCormack and George Underwood, two of his most enduring companions. The three wore cassocks, surplices, and ruffles for church services, as well as the regular weddings that would become David Bowie's first paid engagements as a performer. 'Not only were you given five shillings - a great figure in those days,' MacCormack explains, 'but if the ceremony took place during the week, you got a day off school.'

Because George Underwood's family resided on the opposite side of Bromley, he attended a different primary school. Tall for his age, good-looking, and with an easy, calm, but passionate air about him, he would become David's childhood best buddy. Their relationship would have its ups and downs, but it would be a formative one in their lives. Rock 'n' roll was the glue that held their bond together.

The most contentious, genre-busting early rock 'n' roller, Richard Penniman, would make a powerful touchstone. Many of David's contemporaries, such as Keith Richards of The Rolling Stones, would identify Muddy Waters and Chuck Berry as heroes; they represented true blues formed deep in the Mississippi Delta. Little Richard was a city boy: he'd established his name in New Orleans, studying crazy artists like Guitar Slim and Esquerita and hanging out in a campy cross-dressing scene where fur-coated queens competed to do the greatest Dinah Washington or Sarah Vaughan imitation. His records were nothing like Muddy's deep, soulful songs of yearning or sexual bravado: they were mini-explosions of sound, cranked up with the city's best session men and designed to pack in as many thrills as possible within the two minutes and thirty seconds allowed by the South's jukebox operators. Richard Penniman's music was packaged in flamboyant flair and vividly colored clothing, not just his innate musicianship or captivating voice. Later, he'd come out as gay; later, he'd find God; and much later, David Bowie's wife would buy one of Richard's suits for her husband. David Jones will cherish the first Little Richard recordings he purchased on Bromley High Street for the rest of his life. Elvis Presley would become another inspiration for David, especially after learning that he shared a birthday with the ultimate white rock 'n' roll legend, but Little Richard would become the cornerstone of David's musical identity.

There were a couple of rock 'n' roll lovers at Burnt Ash - Ian Carfrae, subsequently of the New Vaudeville Band, was chastised by the headmaster for bringing 'Rock Around the Clock' into 1955's Christmastime 'gramophone-listening' sessions. While David later became more well-known, George Underwood was the first to get his rock 'n' roll act together. By the time he met David, who possessed a ukulele and had a strong desire to be in a band, he'd already purchased a massive Hofner acoustic guitar and joined a duo with a family friend. In the summer of 1958, the two went to the 18th Cub Scouts Summer Camp on the Isle of Wight, about a year after they initially met. 'We put a washboard bass and David's ukulele in the back of the van and managed to conjure up a couple of tunes around the campfire. That was our first public appearance. We had no claim to virtuosity, but we wanted to sing.'

That shaky first performance, with David playing and George singing, was not the only rite of passage that year. David had taken his 11-plus exam the previous autumn, determining his prospective school. The Burnt Ash students were well prepared, and David and most of his pals went under the watchful eye of Mrs Baldry, David's esteemed and feared teacher. The strict pecking order of schools in the area began with Beckenham and Bromley Grammar at the top, followed by Bromley Technical School - which opened in 1959 and was intended for future commercial artists and engineers - and Quernmore Secondary Modern at the rear. Later in life, David would encourage one of his closest friends to "do the opposite action," which he first did at the age of eleven. Despite the fact that David's grades were adequate for the grammar school, he chose Bromley Tech and persuaded his parents to back his decision.

George Underwood, who was also headed to Bromley Tech, was probably a source of inspiration for this daring action. Because of the Tech's connections with the adjacent Bromley College of Art, he would also be part of a larger network of art school students who would come to define post-war Britain. Contemporaries and near neighbors, such as Keith Richards of the Stones and Dick Taylor of The Pretty Things - dubbed "the war babies" by Richards - were already on the same path. The idea that a generation of children may make a career via art was unique, having emerged from the dramatic revamping of the British educational system in 1944. The art college system established Britain's future prominence in art, advertising, publishing, film, and fashion. As other former students have pointed out, art college taught them that, rather than working in an office or factory, they could make a life with just their "ideas." This liberation was all the more potent because it was linked with a tenacious postwar work ethic. 'We understood then,' explains David's friend Dorothy Bass, 'that after two years at art college, you would have to pay your dues.'

With the exception of the art department, which was housed in a custom-designed facility with north-facing windows to provide greater natural light for painting, the quality of teaching at Bromley Tech was varied. Owen Frampton, the department head, was unquestionably the most well-liked teacher at the school. He was enthusiastic - David recalls him as 'an great art teacher and an inspiration' - but not a pushover. Owen, or 'Ossy,' not only had a keen eye for art, but could also see mischief, according to John Edmonds, a student who recalls throwing a snowball at a teacher unnoticed, only to discover later, when hauled out of class, that the beady-eyed Head of Art had witnessed the occurrence. 'I did develop respect for both his eyesight and his slipper skills,' he recalls ruefully.

David paid close attention in Owen's painting lessons, sketching with charcoals or simply hanging around in the art department, but his interest in other topics waned year by year, to the point that his school report labeled him as a 'lovely idler' in his third year. At fourteen, he had fallen to the passions that would define his life for the next few years: music and females. After school, he would feed both of his addictions at Medhurst's department store on Bromley High Street, a vast Victorian structure that carried furniture and other household items as well as one of south London's top phonograph sections. The gramophone division was handled by a tastefully gay pair named Charles and Jim and was housed in a long, narrow passageway. They carried the usual chart songs and sheet music, but they were also fans of new jazz music and specialized in American imports. David began to appear most afternoons after school to listen to new releases at their listening booth. His passion for music had turned into an obsession, and as time passed, his choices became increasingly broad - encouraged by Terry, his record collection grew to include jazz recordings by Charlie Parker and Charles Mingus. He quickly became a regular, and Jim, the youngest of the two proprietors, and Jane Green, the assistant, would let him have albums at a discount. She quickly 'developed a like' to David. 'Whenever I came in after school, which was most afternoons, she'd let me play records in the "sound booth" until they closed at 5.30. Jane would frequently join me, and we would smooch to the music of Ray Charles or Eddie Cochran. This was quite exciting because I was thirteen or fourteen at the time, and she was a womanly seventeen. 'She was my first older woman.'

Almost all Bromley Tech students from this era appear to remember George and David as a couple, with George being the better remembered of the two. David was exuberant, loving, and expansive; he was cool - people generally noticed his clothes, hair, and things, rather than his personality. He was polite to younger kids in later years, when his first band became recognized around school, but several of his contemporaries echo the opinion of Len Routledge, who says, 'I guess I envied him, or loathed him, as kids do. Because he had a better lifestyle than us, and a father who would bring him things that none of us could have imagined: a whole American football kit, a saxophone, and so on. I honestly liked what he accomplished... But his fortunate circumstances stood in stark contrast to those of myself and many of the other lads.'

The Joneses' former modest existence stood in stark contrast. Haywood's generosity - bordering on profligacy - with money grew as his career at Barnardo's advanced. A few friends recall David's purchase of his American football gear, but much more recall David carrying a saxophone about the Tech. He had hoped for a baritone sax, but had to settle for a Grafton alto, a less expensive but nonetheless beautiful cream plastic Art-Deco concoction purchased by Haywood circa 1960. David was able to 'blame' tuition from baritone player Ronnie Ross, who'd played with bandleader Ted Heath and other big bands and lived nearby, for a brief time. Although the artistic worth of the eight or so lessons was probably small, Ronnie's value for name-dropping purposes was incalculable, and most likely assisted David in landing a Saturday morning employment at Furlong's, the record and instrument store in Bromley South. This tiny music shop, run by a pipe-smoking, trumpet-playing trad jazz fan, was a Mecca in Bromley's tiny musical landscape, its noticeboard providing a hotline to news of local bands' formation and dissolution, while David's new role - of introducing customers to 'new sounds' - helped fuel a new credibility in the music community and, equally importantly, with local girls.

Even if colleagues such as George Underwood overshadowed David as a musician, his confidence drew attention to him. The most well-known example was a school excursion to Spain during the Easter holidays in 1960, which was practically everyone's first venture outside of England. Many families were unable to afford the trip, but David was among the first, and youngest, to sign up. The tiny group took the ferry to Dieppe and then a coach to Spain. They went there to see a bullfight, stare at Franco's armed army, and complain about the hot foreign food. Jones spent much of the day with the local talent, 'off chatting to the females,' according to classmate Richard Comben. The school magazine made a reference to 'Don Jones, the lover, last seen pursued by thirteen senoritas' in honor of David's prowess.

David describes his behavior after discovering girls as 'awful,' and he is the archetypal smooth operator. But, according to Jan Powling, he was anything but to Bromley's female population: 'He was lovely, engaging - not at all any kind of show-off.' She knew David from Burnt Ash Junior, and David asked her out on a date around their third year of high school. As was customary, he called Mr Powling a day or two before the expedition, which had become a double date at some point. So a party of four adolescents boarded the 94 bus to the Bromley Odeon cinema: David was accompanied by Nick, a Bromley Tech acquaintance, and Jan was accompanied by Deirdre, a Burnt Ash Secondary girls school buddy. Jan laments that Deirdre was one of the most popular females in her year, with a blonde haircut and contemporary clothes. By the end of the evening, David was leaving with Deirdre, while Jan was coupled with Nicholas. 'But I don't blame David,' she continues generously,'she was one of the prettiest girls we know.'

Not everyone was as understanding of David's newfound jack-the-lad behavior. One instance of David's deception would become legendary in Bromley Tech mythology, and later in rock 'n' roll history, since it would leave David marked out: an outward manifestation of what was later assumed to be his extraterrestrial nature.

George Underwood was part of the famous brawl, which is unexpected given that he is the most amiable and mild-mannered of personalities. However, in the spring of 1962, when both boys were fifteen, he was incited to violence by an act of plain skulduggery committed by a buddy. George had set up a date with Carol Goldsmith, a Bromley schoolgirl, only for David to tell him she had changed her mind and wouldn't be coming. Soon after, George realized that David, who had a crush on Carol, had lied - Carol had waited for George in vain before returning home after an hour or so, unhappy that she'd been dumped. David's aim was to swoop in on the abandoned girl, but when Underwood found out, they got into a fight. Enraged, Underwood punched his friend in the eye, scratching his eyeball in the process. 'It was simply unfortunate. I didn't have a compass, a battery, or any of the other items I was supposed to have - I didn't even wear a ring, though something must have caught my attention. I'm not sure how it managed to cause such severe damage to his eye... I didn't intend for it to be that way.'

The devastation was severe. David was transported to the hospital, and his classmates were informed that he was in danger of losing sight in his left eye. Underwood was humiliated when he learned that Haywood and Peggy Jones were thinking about charging him with assault. With David gone from school for several weeks, George mustered the nerve to visit Haywood. 'I wanted to convince him it wasn't on purpose. For God's sake, I didn't want to maim him!' The injury to David's eye caused paralysis of the muscles that contract the iris, causing the pupil to be permanently dilated and seem to be a different color than his other eye. His depth perception has also been harmed. 'It gave me a goofy sense of perspective,' David subsequently explained. 'When I'm driving, for example, cars don't approach me; they just get bigger.' It took weeks for David to return to Bromley Tech, and at least a month for him to speak with George (Haywood would eventually forgive him, but it took time). Because of the schism, David missed out on a watershed moment: the debut of rock 'n' roll at Bromley Tech in April 1962. Owen Frampton, who oversaw the lights and the PA system, was a significant element in the talent event. The first half included his son's band, The Little Ravens, sandwiched between a magician and a dancing couple. After the intermission, Underwood's band, George and the Dragons, performed a louder, more rowdy act than Frampton junior's:'very avant-garde for the period,' says Pete Goodchild, who was in the audience.

Only a few weeks later, on June 12, 1962, David Bowie gave his first public performance at the Bromley Tech PTA School Fête. This was the Tech's largest summertime event to date; the PTA purchased a new PA system for the occasion, and over 4,000 parents and townspeople attended. However, no one got to hear David's Joe Brown impression that day because the Kon-Rads concert was entirely instrumental.

David stood with his cream sax hung to one side, next to George Underwood, who played out Shadows' riffs on his Hofner guitar, his hair arranged in a blonde quiff. According to classmate Nick Brookes, David appeared "cool and well dressed." It was an amazing start, but the majority of the crowd agreed on who would go on to stardom: David's taller, better-looking, more popular friend. 'It was George who was the singer, and he did a terrific Elvis impression,' says Tech student Roger Bevan, who remembers Underwood's black, shiny hair and Elvis smirk as well as many other students. 'Everyone thought he was going to be.

Chapter 2: Considering Me

London, 1964, has been immortalized in popular history as swinging and racy, with its happy pulse throbbing to the throb of Jaguar engines and pill-popping Mod songs, pulsing with the illegal joys of cheap sex and gangster cool. In actuality, this beautiful state of affairs was only available to a small handful of insiders. One of them was David Jones. That fateful year, David Jones sashayed boldly into the heart of swinging London, hanging out with the scene's hippest stars and partaking in the shag-tastic promiscuity, convincing many that he had a better right to be there than they did. Within a year, he had established himself as a prominent Face in the scene, distinguished in every way save one: music.

The tenacity with which the seventeen-year-old planned his next career move demonstrated exactly how he operated. On July 19, 1964, he walked into the smoke-filled living room of a suburban semi in Coxheath, Kent, and surprised the residents, a six-piece called The Manish Boys, who'd assumed the 'amazing' singer Les Conn had told them about was David Jones, a black R&B singer who could give their horn-heavy blues vital grit and credibility. A blond, slender, suede-booted teenager strolled in via the sliding picture windows, flanked by the quick-talking Conn. They were even more startled when they discovered they'd engaged him as their singer about a half-hour later.

The band was centered around Solly and Rodriguez, both of whom were three years older than David - or Davie, as he called himself. John Watson sang and played the bass. Johnny Flux, the band's guitarist, arrived a fortnight before David and was another natural-born hustler who had previously sold newspaper advertising space (and went on to create the kids' TV robot Metal Mickey). Woolf Byrne, on baritone sax, also drove and maintained the band's old Bedford van, and drummer Mick Whitehead had walked out on his apprenticeship as a barber.

The band was pleased by David's claims that he was creating his own songs during that first meeting, even though the sole song he played,

'Don't Try to Stop Me,' sounded suspiciously like a Marvin Gaye number. David was open about suggesting new material, most notably from James Brown's Live at the Apollo; The Manish Boys' own set soon included Ray Charles ('What'd I Say'), Solomon Burke ('Stupidity'), and even Conway Twitty ('Make Me Know Your Mind'), and they hit the road with their new singer in August.

Those early months with The Manish Boys were perplexing, carefree, and rarely dull. The band shared clothes and slept on friends' floors while begging their parents for food, housing, and money. David reinvented his own life this summer. He'd resigned his work at Nevin D. Hirst by this point, and seemed to be basing his new persona on the beat novels he was reading. He was the most migratory of the group; whereas the others might spend a day away from home, he would spend a week hanging out with buddies. This chimed in with his frequent mentions of Dylan, Jack Kerouac, and J. Saunders Redding's On Being Negro in America, one of several books he bought in paperback at Bromley South Station. Throughout their gigs, practice sessions at Charlie Chester's Casino or a labyrinth of rooms and brothels on Windmill Street, or socializing at the Regency Club - a favorite for the Kray Twins - The Manish Boys built an intense, jovial relationship, like warriors on a grueling mission. Their closeness extended to the girls who were everywhere that autumn of 1964, their names and phone numbers scribbled in pink lipstick all over the band's green Bedford van. While his friends were packing up amplifiers and equipment at the end of a gig, David was out on the dancefloor, chatting up his female audience: 'getting in there first,' as the jargon went.

Les Conn had rejected to take his managing cut of the band's occasional live earnings after reuniting David with The Manish Boys, but he still hustled on their behalf. At the end of September, he landed an audition with Mickie Most, who, in the aftermath of The Animals' 'House of the Rising Sun,' was perhaps London's largest independent producer. The band performed a handful of songs after setting up in one of their usual haunts, comedian Charlie Chesters casino on Archer Street. Most made his decision on the spot, as was his custom, asking, 'Do you want to record for me, boys?' 'Yes!' they exclaimed in unison.

According to Woolf, this was the most powerful indication that the band's youngest member was "mature beyond his years." He could deduce the politics of a gathering well before his pals. The Manish Boys auditioned at the London Palladium that winter, hoping to land a residency at Hamburg's famed Star Club.

The set had gone well, and Bob Solly watched as the Star Club's promoter summoned David. Before David returned to the stage, the two exchanged a few words and grins. 'What did he say?' Solly inquired.

"Which way do you swing, Davie, boys or girls?" he inquired. David informed him.
'What exactly did you say?'
'Oh, I told him, "Boys, of course"!'

The anecdote demonstrated his growing talent for securing a deal, and it came as no surprise when they learned that the audition had gone well and that they would be booked into the Star Club the following summer. When Woolf and David were drinking coffee in La Gioconda, a chic wood-paneled coffee cafe on Denmark Street that was a favorite musicians' hangout, a BBC researcher approached them and asked if their long hair had ever given them issues. Both of them desired a TV appearance and a five-guinea fee, but it was David who devised the concept of a 'League for the Protection of Animal Filament' - a support group for downtrodden longhairs that existed purely in his mind.

That unexpected contact with the researcher resulted in a 92-second interview on Tonight with Cliff Michelmore, which aired on November 12, 1964, and was destined to be one of David's great TV appearances - because he does such a perfect, funny job of selling nothing.

John Watson, the other singer for the Manish Boys, was three years older, had a greater voice, experience, and education, but was absolutely invisible in comparison to his younger colleague. Although manager Ken Pitt would later instruct David Bowie on how to deal with the media, this little segment, now a YouTube classic, indicates Pitt was working with a natural. Whereas Davie Jones' debut as a vocalist was at best mediocre, his debut as a self-publicist was flawless.

The tour provided an ideal occasion to test a new song, 'Pity the Fool,' which Shel Talmy, an American producer who shared an office building with Howes, chose as the band's debut single. Talmy, a one-time kid prodigy who'd starred on NBC's Quiz Kids, had 'bullshitted' his way into the UK by claiming to have produced The Beach Boys, then backed up his claim with a string of super-compressed high-energy songs for The Who and The Kinks. The band and their singer piqued Shel's interest: 'Les Conn told me I should listen to this man - and Les was correct, he always had a fantastic ear for talent.'

Despite their bravado, The Manish Boys were frightened during their session on January 15, 1965, at London's IBC studio. 'But David was obviously not intimidated,' recalls Talmy. 'That was what I liked about him.' In reality, David's singing has improved since his dismal debut. The vocals, confident and impassioned, with superb microphone technique, show a man who, like Shel Talmy, lied his way into a job - and then delivered.

Clunky, unsophisticated, and all the better for it, the song became an underappreciated masterpiece of British blues, which Jimmy Page recognized right immediately. 'Good session,' he said as he packed up his Fender Telecaster, 'but I don't think it's a hit.' He lessened the impact by offering a riff he'd played while warming up, assuring David he might use it in one of his own songs ('The Supermen' appeared years later). David was already telling people about his job as a songwriter, though based on the B-side of their record, 'Take My Tip,' he didn't have much of a future. The song was an unremarkable parody of Georgie Fame, one of the band's current obsessions, set to a clunky, clichéd chord sequence and distinguished mainly by complicated lyrics.

The slow death of The Manish Boys was made more agonizing for David by his friend George Underwood's meteoric rise. Les Conn had kept battling for George, whom he saw as "just as talented as David." And he was a much kinder guy; he didn't have the "I'm the cat's whiskers' ' [mentality]. Les had taken both George and David to see Mickie Most, who simply liked George better'. Most treated Underwood like a son, chauffeuring him around town in his Rolls Royce and giving him advice on life, money, and the music business before deciding he needed a more glamorous moniker. Underwood was so given the stage name Calvin James, after Mickie's son Calvin, and was pampered like a rock star every time he visited Most's record label, RAK. David did not appear to be pleased with his friend's achievement. When they ran into each other on Bromley High Street, George felt David's eyes on him like daggers.

The last few Manish Boys gigs were riotous: on 13 March, David and Johnny Flux, who'd started camping it up together more and more after their Gillingham adventure, were barred from entering the venue. Their final gig was at Bletchley on April 24, and the band returned to Maidstone without David, who had gone missing with a female fan who was hosting a party in the town. There were no formal goodbyes: the next time Solly and Rodriguez saw David, he was in Shel Talmy's office, clearly plotting something new. And there would be no dispute about who would get top billing this time.

The three had just been hanging out on Denmark Street for about a week when they saw the young David Jones in La Gioconda. 'Blimey,' Denis Taylor exclaims, 'there goes Keith Relf of The Yardbirds!' The band had advertised for a singer and held tryouts at La Discotheque on Wardour Street, a regular hotspot where they'd performed as a five-piece. 'But the odd part was that he came along with an alto sax, so we believed he was a saxophonist,' he says.

David had brought along moral support in the form of vocalist Stevie Marriott, whom he had met earlier that year at a Manish Boys rehearsal. A jam session ensued, using a funky version of Little Richard's 'Rip it Up' as the foundation. 'Steve was fantastic,' Taylor recalls, 'perhaps a better singer than David.'

Then, perplexingly, Stevie left and David took the mic, sounding "exactly like Keith Relf" on their cover of The Yardbirds' "I Wish

You Would." He quickly persuaded The Lower Third of his superb connections. 'He told us a few trade secrets - I got the idea that Shel had taught him a lot. And he looked fantastic. So we made the decision to bring him in.'

The meeting took place just as The Manish Boys were crumbling under the weight of their defeat. David's demeanor showed no sign of this; in fact, his confidence had grown. Davie Jones had shared vocals and band leadership in both The King Bees and The Manish Boys. With The Lower Third, the eighteen-year-old took creative leadership, pushing Taylor, who was three years older at the time, to learn new songs while also supporting David with his own creations. Their cranked-up version of 'I Wish You Would' became a live staple; David brilliantly imitated Keith Relf's vocal manner - he'd also started playing the harmonica for an even better carbon copy. Other clear influences included The Kinks, whose song 'All Day and All of the Night' was also used, and The Who. David saw The Lower Third multiple times during his first few months with them and pressed Taylor to adopt a similar grandiose guitar tone. 'It was a learning curve,' Taylor shudders still.

True to tradition, David had already written a press statement describing how the new band, Davie Jones and The Lower Third, featured 'TEA-CUP on lead, DEATH on bass, and LES on drums' within a few weeks of joining the band. The one-page document reminded readers of "the legendary Banned Hair tale" and promised another appearance on Gadzooks, as well as a new track, "Born of the Night," that was "destined to rush up the charts." (The song was a demo recorded in a friend's practice space and was never released.)

David appeared emancipated now that he'd taken over leadership of a band; there was an irresistible enthusiasm to the way he'd throw himself into a project. Davie was presenting himself as a songwriter just eight or ten weeks after obtaining his first composition credit with 'Take My Tip,' popping in at Shel's studio to demo stuff, and pitching songs to other performers. Les Conn, who had organized a Kenny Miller recording of 'Take My Tip' in February, had covered his first tune. Most of those early songs were terrible, but he kept sending them in; aesthetically, they ranged from Dylan impersonations to Gene Pitney knock-offs. Talmy observed that David'sounded like a lot of different people at different times' and that a lot of the content was 'not terrific' - yet there was something about David that he loved; like many, he was drawn to David's 'energy,' the way he constantly came up with ideas. Whereas George Underwood was devastated by losses, David seemed unaffected by them; the brief taste of success he'd had so far merely fuelled his thirst for more. Today, he emphasizes that such disappointments 'never, ever' made him feel negative, 'since I still liked the process. Writing and recording were enjoyable activities for me as a child. "God, I don't think anything is ever going to happen for me," I could have thought, but I'd bounce back quite quickly.

As David spent more time in the West End, particularly around Denmark St, he began to hang out at the FD&H publishing firm and record shop on Charing Cross Road, strumming guitars or speaking with shop manager Wayne Bardell, with whom he became friends. Bardell had accompanied David to the first Manish Boys recording session and, like many others, had seen David was very confident, without being arrogant - this was not a person who felt agitated'. He saw David go from being a member of The Manish Boys' band to being the leader of The Lower Third. Then, as David entered the establishment and sat behind the counter, he made a very strange remark. 'It was, like, "Wayne?" I'm not going to talk to anyone when I'm famous, not even the band." It was an odd thing to say, but it resonated with me.' Only then did he realize how 'nice' David was all the time. But I guess he never really gave anything away.'

Drummer Les Mighall went back to Margate for the weekend a few weeks after David joined The Lower Third and never returned. David found a new drummer, Phil Lancaster, who helped the band complete its change into a cranked-up, super-violent style greatly influenced by The Who, a sound developed throughout the band's hectic summer, which was spent gigging in Margate and other southeast resorts.

Working on tunes and hanging out with David in their London flat, Plaistow Grove, or Margate was a delightful era for the band and David. David appeared to be a natural band member, always up for a laugh and understanding when to become serious. On the side, David and Denis worked on advertisements for Youthquake Clothing and Puritan, both of which were created and recorded in their Who-influenced manner at RG Jones Studio in Wimbledon, where David made the majority of his recordings until 1966.

With his now-familiar inventiveness, David had a substitute in mind: Ralph Horton, a regular at La Gioconda. Over the next year, Horton rose to prominence. There was never any question about his dedication. 'He would have done anything to advance David's career,' says coworker John Hutchinson,'so he might have been a terrific manager.' However, Horton's time with David was dominated by financial problems and disagreements with David's musicians, who, like Denis Taylor, "didn't like Ralph from the start." Graham Rivens, bassist, is even more vehement: 'I despised him. It wasn't just that he was a fucking poofta; I despised him in every way.'

Horton arrived on the scene just as EMI put pressure on Shel Talmy, who already had enough on his plate with The Kinks and The Who, to terminate David's singles deal. 'David was fine but not great,' the producer says. 'He was going to improve, but he wasn't in the same category as Pete Townshend or Ray Davies. EMI simply thought that the market was not buying it.' The divorce was cordial. Horton told David that he could find another deal; yet, the ambitious manager was aware of his own limits, as on September 15th, Horton called a well-known publicist named Ken Pitt to explore incorporating him in David's management. Pitt stated that he was too busy to take on another client, and that Davie Jones' name was a problem because he already knew David Jones who went on to join the Monkees, as well as the south London war poet and painter of the same name.

Horton refused to give up on Pitt and kept calling him. Pitt's misgivings over David's name were also taken seriously by him. David, it turned out, had already planned an alternative. He'd already tried on other names for size, including his saxophone name, David Jay. He had seen the film The Alamo during his Kon-Rads era and had gotten captivated with the figure played by Richard Widmark: Jim Bowie. 'In the dressing room, he proclaimed himself Bowie at least once,' says Kon-Rads drummer David Hadfield, 'and started dressing in this tasseled leather jacket.' Horton wrote to Pitt the day after their original phone call, notifying him that his protégé would now be known as David Bowie. Everyone involved was excited about the new moniker, though it would undoubtedly spark debate in playgrounds and sixth-form common rooms over the next decade. David always pronounced the name to rhyme with Snowy, TinTin's beloved terrier, however many Northern colleagues pronounced it 'Bow' to rhyme with 'plough'.

The new name embodied David's ambitions of splendor and stardom, while also helping him consign his previous, unsuccessful single to history. Mark Feld followed in his footsteps, recording his debut song at Decca Studio 2. By the time 'The Wizard' was released on November 19, Mark had renamed himself Marc Bolan and crafted an engagingly absurd press statement about a wizard-inspired vacation to Paris with Les Conn's support. David and Marc, both friends and adversaries, kept a careful eye on each other's growth.

Between gigs, David worked on tunes, frequently with the entire band crowded inside his Plaistow Grove bedroom. Today, David expresses fears that he would never admit to himself back then: 'I didn't know how to create a song, and I wasn't very good at it. I had no inherent talents... and the only way I could learn was to see how others did it. 'I wasn't one of those people who came out of the womb dancing like Marc - I was bumbling around,' he explains. But he persisted, humming phrases and tunes that Denis Taylor had to interpret, altering the chords until they found one that David loved. It was laborious work, like navigating a maze in the dark. David 'wanted the music done right soon - but he was also very patient, and this would go on for days,' Taylor explains. On 'You've Got a Habit of Leaving Me,' David just instructed Denis to move his hand up and down the fretboard. They incorporated additional tricks, such as ninths, sevenths, and minor chords, which added intricacy to David's content. 'Some of it was quite morbid. 'Quite miserable,' Taylor admits. Throughout the end of 1965, David worked on 'The London youths,' a vignette of pill-popping youths dressed in their finery that was clearly influenced by Ray Davies' songs like 'See My Friends'.

'The London Boys' was an anthem for a new generation of kids, an obvious ancestor of Bowie epics like 'Lady Stardust' and 'All the Young Dudes': a celebration of otherness, right down to the clothing, the hint of homo-eroticism, and the evocation of Judy Garland in its 'too late now, 'cause you're on the run' climax. Its combination of world-weariness and naiveté defines the persona that David would assume for a decade or more: a man-child, someone who as a youngster seemed unusually serene and mature, yet as an adult appeared waif-like, with a juvenile earnestness. David Bowie's androgyny would be extensively - and rightfully - celebrated in later years, but this man-child aura was an equally significant component of his personal, often devastating charm.

'The London Boys' foreshadowed another common Bowie technique: riding along with a youth movement while distancing himself from it. David was a latecomer to the Mod movement, as he was to others, behind pioneers like Marc Bolan, who'd made his mark early in a seven-page profile in Town magazine back in September 1962, taken by famed war photographer Don McCullin. Although he arrived late, David was immediately accepted by Mod pioneers such as Jeff Dexter, the DJ and leading Face who had been comparing lapels and partings with Marc Bolan for years. 'I saw David at the Bromel Club in 1964, and he was bright.' Marc and David's passion with clothes solidified their connection; together, they explored Carnaby Street, hunting for rejected garments in the bins outside the boutiques.

More importantly, David joined forces with the band that would become the main lights of the Mod movement for only a few weeks. David had continued to hang out with Steve Marriott at La Gioconda in the days following his Lower Third audition, and when Marriott linked up with the future Small Faces, David sat in on their practices and helped them lug their gear around. He sang backup vocals on the first few gigs. 'He was fantastic,' drummer Kenney Jones says. 'He was definitely one of us. A fantastic Mod, with a tremendous hairdo, a great personality, and a great look - he was very conscious of his image.' David became the 'fifth Small Face' during this time. However, he would never acknowledge this exciting cooperation with the Small Faces because it failed due to the flaw that has afflicted most of his endeavors, notably his shameless replication of others' styles. 'We weren't into protest songs, but David was,' Jones explains. We eventually thought he was too Dylanesque.'

The band's rejection must have been a tremendous blow, for he never mentioned it to any of his confidants. Jones, who went on to play with both the Faces and The Who, adds, 'I still think about David, personally, and latch on to those recollections of our misspent youth.' Despite the fact that David never made public his involvement with the Small Faces, he remained respectful of Stevie Marriott, who, powered by his wonderful voice and songwriting combination with bassist Ronnie Lane, would eventually acquire the renown that David craved.

Despite these setbacks, Bowie's brief stint as a Mod was vital, as the young movement formed all of the fundamental beliefs that enraged Britain in 1972. In many ways, seventies glam was modernism taken to its logical conclusion, and it's no accident that the founding trio of glam - Bowie, Bolan, and Bryan Ferry - were all definitive Mods. (The only philosophical difference was that the Mod ideal was exclusive, targeted only at peers, whereas glam was supposed to be publicized - knowingly pimped, with a sardonic grin.) The idea of preening, peacock guys bonding with fellow males over a side-vent or suit lining, oblivious to the disdain of outsiders, was shocking - and compelling - in 1964, when simply wearing a pink shirt was a daring statement. There were no prominent role models to point to to deflect the disdain of the un-hip; you were on your own separate from your peers. Mod was the province of the unabashed narcissist, and David Bowie and Marc Bolan became two of London's most dedicated narcissists.

Mod and 'The London Boys' had a distinct gay vibe to them. The city's Mod and gay communities frequented the same clubs and shared many beliefs. The Scene in neighboring Ham Yard was nominally Mod, and Le Duce on D'Arblay Street was nominally gay, yet you could pose or dance to Bluebeat in either. In 1964 and 1965, there were plenty of Mod boys who experimented with their sexuality as well as their attire in Soho, and David was one among them.

This was an exciting time for both Berry and David. 'Until 1964, life appeared black and white. Then it exploded with color.' Like many of his generation, his sex life was a part of his protest against monochrome, straight-laced norms. 'They were amazing times,' he says. 'I knew I was bisexual since I had a girlfriend and liked other people - then we all decided, Who cares? 'Anything is possible!'

'Mostly, we'd speak about things,' David says of his and Mike's friendship, which included a sexual element. We chatted about music, politics, and what was going on in Cuba at the time he was semi-straight and semi-gay - none of us knew whether we'd be living the next year. Or we'd argue over whether we liked him or her, who had whom, and who was speaking the truth.'

David was calm, playful, and witty, and he had a waif-like appearance. And, of course, those eyes caught your attention right immediately; they were unforgettable.' David's superb looks allowed him to easily move in and out of the gay-oriented scene; he flaunted his campiness, but it was all in good fun. In fact, his campiness aided him in attracting more girls. He was primarily straight; on occasion, he'd go on dates with Dana Gillespie, a sixteen-year-old former public schoolgirl with an amazing cleavage whom he'd met during The Manish Boys' final days; Dana would occasionally bring her friend Sarah Troupe along for a double date. David had also dated Annie Howes, the promoter's daughter, but it appeared to his pals that he 'had a female in every port,' as Denis Taylor puts it. 'Somewhere we went, a bird would appear.'

Many of Ralph Horton's ties revolved around the Marquee and Radio London, both of which had a sizable gay population, all of whom were fascinated by David's friendship with Horton. Simon Napier-Bell stated on his website in 2006, in a typically ridiculous narrative, that Horton had offered him David's sexual favors in exchange for a co-management arrangement. Whatever Horton promised, David's confidantes, such as Mike Berry, assert, "It would never have happened in a million years." David was always in command of what he desired.'

Worse, there was an air of sleaze about Horton's financial dealings, exemplified by a deal he made in November 1965 with a London businessman, Ray Cook, to borrow £1500 - a figure worth approximately £30,000 in today's currency. A hazy contract claimed that the money would be returned after David earned more than £100 per week. Ken Pitt, who took over as Bowie's next manager and had to untangle these financial complexities, is not alone in believing Cook was duped. 'I felt bad for him. It was a bad situation.'

Horton's one coup was landing a new recording deal with Tony Hatch, whom he met through Denny Laine. Hatch, the Pye label's house producer, went on to become one of the UK's most well-known producers - the Simon Cowell of the 1970s - thanks to his participation on the New Faces talent show. 'But I saw he wasn't "top echelon" - he was still in the junior league,' he said of Horton. And I expected a new manager to arrive soon if David had a hit.'

Hatch, on the other hand, was impressed with David, particularly because he wrote his own songs. Pye was an odd mash-up of the Polygon and Nixa labels that Hatch had joined as a part-time producer, arranging A&R meetings in the afternoons so he could fulfill his National Service as arranger for the Coldstream Guards (another Pye act) in the mornings. He had a massive workload, so the fact that he didn't have to source stuff for David was critical. 'What struck me was that he had a lot of tunes - various songs.' Hatch went to see The Lower Third at the Marquee to familiarize himself with the subject. 'I recall "The London Boys" - there were a lot of songs about his upbringing. There was one on the Hackney Marshes that is presumably somewhere in an archive.' (Unfortunately, David's unpublished Pye material appears to have vanished.)

With Hatch's multiple distractions, securing a recording contract took some time; the publishing stayed close to home, with Mike Berry signing him to Sparta for his planned singles. The deal brought in a small advance, and the financial flow supported a season of high living at Horton's Warwick Square flat, complete with costly drinking parties. David purchased a guitar during this high-living phase, and although his playing was, at best, amateurish, he made up tunes like 'It's Lovely to Talk to You' and 'Maid of Bond Street'. The

Lower Third demoed 'The London Boys,' which they thought was a standout tune, in the autumn, but Hatch and his Pye colleagues turned it down at their weekly sales meeting. 'It takes too long to get going,' says Hatch, not the depressing subject matter or references to pill popping. It'll never be a single.'

Its replacement was significantly more succinct, with a simple three-chord chorus taken shamelessly from 'Anyway, Anyhow, Anywhere'. 'Can't Help Thinking About Me' steals the same three-chord trick as 'You've Got a Habit of Leaving Me,' but it makes far better use of it, with that punchy chorus allied to a subtle verse whose minor-key chords perfectly match the foreboding lines of a 'question time that says I brought dishonor'.

The verse alone was a significant advancement in David's work, but it was combined with another complex approach, a pre-chorus passage that builds anticipation ('it's too late now') before the chorus is released. This was a song as story, with one musical vignette leading to the next, a method that became a trademark of David Bowie's famous songs.

The lyrics, too, are nuanced, with indications of a crime that had stained the family name, and a chorus that slightly subverts expectations, for according to pop tradition, the protagonist should have been thinking about a 'you', not 'me'. In many cases, assuming David is the target of his own lyrics is overly simplistic, but here, the accusation of blackening the family name matches some of Peggy's objections. She'd been cordial to The Manish Boys, lovely well-spoken middle-class men, but she'd lost patience with David's artistic ambitions and had a cynical disdain of his Margate pals. 'She didn't like us at all,' Denis Taylor laments. 'I recall her saying to me, "You're leading my boy astray - he was never like this before."

The record was released on January 14, 1966, just one week after David turned nineteen. Ralph Horton had borrowed more money from Raymond Cook for a launch party and to assist in getting the single into the charts. The band walked through nearby Hyde Park to get there, while David took a ride in Ralph's Jaguar, and all the musicians dressed up and mingled with the Pye staff and celebrities, the most famous of whom was Freddie Lennon, John Lennon's incorrigible absentee father, who was enjoying a brief flurry of notoriety. 'It was a really strange party,' Taylor says. 'Freddie Lennon, this strange old geezer, a little tipsy, roaming around saying "Do you know who I am?"'

That night, David was effervescent, pleasant with The Lower Third - 'like we were a legitimate band' - meeting and greeting small industry figures and exclaiming to his band, 'This is it!' He relished being at the center of the action, dashing off to woo one gaggle of guests after another, flirting with the Pye secretaries, and assuming an accommodating, likely-lad demeanor with the company's suited officials. He'd just turned nineteen, had released his first hit single, and was certain that this was it.

Chapter 3: Every Madman

It was their Graceland: the opulent, rambling, and slightly deteriorating mansion where David and Angela Bowie reveled in marital bliss, interior design, and sexual frolics. Innocent adolescent American ladies would stroll in and fantasize about being imprisoned in a re-imagined Victorian melodrama; cynical journalists would approach its enormous hallway and be overwhelmed by the Bowie mystique. It was a place where the musical and fashion values of a whole decade would be reshaped.

Angie first noticed Haddon Hall, located at 240 Southend Road in Beckenham, in the summer of 1969. Beckenham, a comparatively green and beautiful suburb best known as the birthplace of Enid Blyton, was just down the road from Bromley. Angie and David arranged to move into Flat 7 in early September and settle in by the end of the month. The structure was the embodiment of collapsing magnificence, an extravagant High-Victorian family mansion that reminded resident John Cambridge of Elvis Presley's enormous Memphis residence.

The building was divided into flats; David and Angie's flat was on the ground floor, but they also had access to the staircase, which led visitors up to a small half-landing dominated by a magnificent Gothic stained-glass window; from there, the staircase divided, ascending to a gallery at first-floor level, which gave on to a set of sealed-up doorways, later commandeered as sleeping space. Tony Visconti and his girlfriend Liz moved into Haddon Hall in December, taking the back bedroom on the ground floor and sharing a huge living room with David and Angie, complete with a lavish open fireplace; Tony soon persuaded Mr Hoys, the house's owner, to let him build a rehearsal space in the basement.

Royalties from the 'Space Oddity' single, which had sold 138,656 copies in the UK by January, trickled in gradually, but the success of the record pushed up the pay for David's live bookings to a fantastic £100 or more. For the first time in his life, David was flush and spent money like a duck to water. After passing his driving test and returning his father's Fiat to Peggy, he purchased a Rover 100 with luxurious leather seats and a walnut dashboard, while he and Angie became regulars at the antique shops on Old Kent and Tower Bridge Roads, where they purchased Art Deco lamps, William Morris screens, and mahogany chests of drawers.

Angie was crowned queen to Bowie's king with the establishment of their own palace at Haddon Hall. It was an extraordinarily quick rise to prominence, but it came as little surprise to her most recent associates. Mary Angela Barnett, born in Cyprus in 1950 to an American mining engineer father and a Polish mother, and educated at a British boarding school in Montreux, Switzerland, was self-sufficient, vivacious, and seductively noisy. She delighted in telling listeners about her scandalous expulsion from Connecticut College for Women for a lesbian romance, and to most Brits - in the days before cheap transatlantic travel - she appeared ravishingly international. She was raised in a cultured, international environment and was equally at ease scouring Haddon Hall's wooden floorboards to remove the odor of cat pee as she was recognizing a real Art Nouveau light fitting from a replica.

'You met Angie before you knew David,' says John Cambridge, starting in the spring of 1970. Their union would always be as public as it was personal, much like celebrity liaisons arranged by Hollywood publicists eager to maximize column inches. Cambridge was one among many who found Angie annoying - 'too forceful and yelling' - and saw firsthand how Angie would force David into actions he wished to avoid, most notably firing Ken Pitt.

The sole new song David wrote during the winter of 1969, 'The Prettiest Star,' was the first public declaration of their love connection. (Absence made his heart grow fonder, because Angie went missing in November to see her parents, partially to avoid Peggy's phone calls accusing her of 'living in sin.') It would be almost unique in Bowie's canon: a traditional love ballad, its lyrics speculating on their future renown as a professional pair, 'you and I shall rise up all the way'.

The squabble revealed the strain that will always exist in David Bowie's friendship with Marc Bolan. Marc had always enjoyed praising David, but after predicting that 'Space Oddity' would be a smash, Marc appeared upset to be proven correct. This was a clear example of how the youthful 'arrogance' Les Conn recalls stemmed from various factors. When his pals did well, David was generally pleased; Marc was not. What Bowie perceived as confidence equated to bravado in Bolan, a distinction for which June Bolan had an explanation, which she communicated with Ray Stevenson. 'She had this theory that Marc had a small dick and David had a monster,' she explained. A lot of their characteristics stem from this: David can enchant the girl and know that he will not disappoint her till the end of this contact. Marc was unable to.'

David put up a fine show of being unfazed by Marc's petulance - he was upbeat on the trip back to Beckenham in his Rover in the early hours of the morning, purchasing a massive Chinese takeaway on the way and putting it all over the dashboard. But, while he may appear serene in the face of such difficulties, his music often suffered from the jumbled mass of people that surrounded him during this time; he relied on others more than most. The Speakeasy show that night exemplified the misunderstanding. Tim Renwick, David's preferred guitarist over Mick Wayne, was called in at the last minute, but found David's inactivity and lack of direction annoying. 'It wasn't as if they said, "Right, here we go." It was more of a "What's next?" followed by nothing. John Cambridge had arrived for a drink at the 'Speak,' along with Junior's Eyes' 'Roger the roadie,' only to be asked at the last minute, 'Do you have your drums?' He luckily kept them in the boot of his Mini Minor. His debut as Bowie's official drummer came as a last-minute request.

The majority of individuals present were unaware that David had a brother, but practically everyone was familiar with Cane Hill. The institution, which opened in 1882, was a massive, purpose-built Gothic building designed to provide a more sympathetic, modern setting for the 'incurably mad,' with wide gardens and outdoor pavilions from which inmates could enjoy views of London. Nonetheless, the structure, situated on a commanding hill in Coulsdon, ten miles south-east of Beckenham, was regarded as a terrifying place, famous locally as the insane asylum that had housed Charlie Chaplin's mother, who had been confined to a padded cell and hosed down with freezing water as a primitive forerunner of electro-shock therapy. The establishment was more progressive in the 1960s, but there was a legitimate concern among convicts and their families that once they passed past its towering gates, they would never return. 'Don't lose your way - they might keep you here,' Hannah Chaplin warned her son when he came to visit her.

about 1969 and 1970, when David first had his own home, he was also able to provide shelter for his half-brother, and Terry could be spotted about Haddon Hall at various occasions after his release from Cane Hill. During this time, he met several of David's closest friends and was cordial, sometimes chatty - especially about football - and sometimes puzzled. In the long run, however, David proved just as incapable of dealing with Terry's condition as his mother.

Those who saw David and Terry together knew that, as Mark Pritchett recalls, 'Terry adored his brother...' and he was a great fellow.' David clearly adored and revered Terry, naming him as the source of many of his significant musical and literary interests on numerous occasions. According to Pritchett, the main emotion Terry instilled in his half-brother was "guilt."

That guilt was justified, according to David's aunt Pat, who publicly rebuked David for his lack of care to Terry in the 1980s: David simply turned his back on his half-brother. To be fair, there was probably not much he could have done. 'I've known some schizophrenics and there isn't much you can do to help - they are how they are and it's dreadful,' says Ray Stevenson, who spent a lot of time at Haddon Hall as Terry's mental health deteriorated. You simply must not think about it. So I'd never criticize him for that.'

Bowie's dread of his family's insanity would become a recurring motif - it's the stuff of classical drama, and it's been a prism through which many have chosen to analyze his career, despite the lack of evidence to back it up. Throughout this time, David was noticeably calm and controlled: he couldn't have appeared more rational. However, as anyone who has been emotionally close to someone suffering from schizophrenia or paranoia knows,'madness' is contagious; reports of a schizophrenic's visions can be more touching, appear more convincing, than true, prosaic events. David felt empathy for his half-brother when he created songs; in ordinary life, David felt impotent. Terry's condition was always an issue that David dealt with in song rather than in reality, which resulted in 'David building up a lot of guilt over him,' explains Mark Pritchett. And I believe the darker songs are in fact tributes to him.'

Tim Renwick was the clear favorite guitarist. But John Cambridge, David's first formal recruit, had another prospect in mind: a tremendously gifted guitarist from his previous band, The Rats: 'I'd been bugging [David and Tony] to no end, so I went down to Hull to locate Mick Ronson. I knew where he worked; I arrived and he's creating this training field; I told him I've got an audition with David Bowie's band in London; it's incredibly fantastic, and it needs a guitarist. And he's off... "Oh, I don't know, I got in with a band in Sweden and was ripped off, and I'm not about to do that again." So I'm thinking to myself, 'I just pestered them two to let me come down here - and now I have to pester him to go up there!'

Cambridge's argument was successful. On 3 February, Ronson attended the band's play at the Marquee; after the show, the guitarist complimented favorably on the performance, as was his wont. 'Mick would claim it was good even if it was garbage,' Cambridge explains. At the venue, the drummer introduced Bowie to Ronson, but David was busy; it wasn't until they all returned to Haddon Hall and Ronson pulled up an acoustic and began to play that Bowie noticed him. 'Everything was starting to come into place at that point,' Tony Visconti says.

Over the previous five or six years, Mick Ronson's career had been intertwined with Bowie's through fellow Yorkshiremen like John Hutchinson, who had shared the bill with The Rats at clubs around the north-east. Born and reared in Hull, once an affluent and confident Victorian city but already gripped by a long-term industrial downturn by the late 1960s, Mick Ronson was a one-of-a-kind artist, cutthroat in terms of musical ambition but amazingly laid-back when it came to furthering his own career.

Keith Herd, a local musician, saw one of Ronson's first tentative gigs with his band The Crestas and ran into the guitarist on a regular basis at Cornell's, a local music store. In 1967, after Herd put up a modest recording studio in his front room, Mick turned up with his new band, The Rats, 'and I couldn't believe how he'd come on'. Ronson had mastered 'heavy guitar,' using the amplifier and power to achieve remarkable sustain while playing a Fender Telecaster. It was the first time I'd heard someone do it.'

The Rats' four-minute mini-opera 'The Rise and Fall of Bernie Gripplestone' was Who-influenced, with Ronson's howling guitar serving as the sole distinguishing feature. Although there are shades of Hendrix, Townshend and Mick's principal guitar idol, Jeff Beck, Ronson's playing was already unique; concise, tough rhythm guitar one moment, wildly fluid lead the next, made all the more thrilling by Ronson's talent for bending a note to scary extremes - a unique trick that, according to bandmate Trevor Bolder, he'd mastered thanks to a fingernail on his left hand that was so tough and hard it was 'almost deformed'. He could bend the string almost all the way across the neck of the guitar by knocking it into a groove on the nail. By the time he picked up a Les Paul Custom from Cornell's and plugged it into his Marshall stack at the end of 1968, he had established himself as Hull's unrivaled guitar hero.

Mick was pleasant, a classic muso, with his flint-sharp face and boney nose: his talk centered around music and ladies; if he saw someone ogling his guitar, he'd nod and encourage them, urging them, 'Go on, have a go.' Then he'd gladly shake the new acquaintance's hand. Musically, he was open-minded, enjoying harmony pop like The Move as well as strong rock. And, like the rest of The Rats, adds bassist Keith 'Ched' Cheeseman, 'he was a piss-taker'. 'Piss-taking' was frequently aimed at recommending that The Rats change their 'winning' formula. By the end of 1969, Cheeseman realized that, while Mick was unquestionably the best musician in Hull when he initially joined the band, younger competition were catching up to him.

Mick Ronson had relished being in his comfort zone with The Rats. But he was yanked out of it by David Bowie and Tony Visconti. That Saturday, he huddled with the pair, frantically learning songs for Jeff Griffin 'In Concert' on Sunday, February 5th. It was a tremendous win for Bowie to headline the new series - Marc Bolan, on the other hand, was a last-minute replacement for half a program - and David's usage of a guitarist he'd seen two days before was a huge risk; an early example of the brilliant gambles that would come to characterize his career.

Another first for Bowie was his use of the BBC to prototype the next phase of his work for the 'In Concert' presentation. There is a fresh roughness and sense of urgency from its opening minutes in front of a small audience at Regent Street's Paris Cinema, with a gritty, solo version of Brel's "Port of Amsterdam." Songs like 'Unwashed and Somewhat Slightly Dazed' sound Dylan-esque and barely worthy - until Ronson hooks his mutant fingernail under the guitar string and, for the first time in Bowie's career, the listener is unsure where the song is going (a feeling shared by Ronson, who gets a couple of chords wrong). Nonetheless, it is his drawn-out, weary guitar work that prompts announcer John Peel to call the song "a bit of a treat."

David appeared to be well aware that he'd rounded a corner. 'You could tell he thought a band would be good for him,' Pritchett adds. During the erratic series of performances that continued into February and March, he was at ease, enjoying his journey to Hull for a show at the university on 6 March, when he hung around in the refectory with a small group of supporters and puzzled students. Angie's presence seemed to be as noticeable to them as the band's. 'David and Angie had the same curly hair, similar slender physique, you know how individuals who appear a little similar to each other might fall in love?' recalled one student who sat at the same table as them.

The failure of the record commemorating his and Angie's love was the sole disappointment in an otherwise wonderful spring for David. 'The Prettiest Star,' released the same day they sat speaking in the refectory, slid into obscurity with less than 1000 copies sold. The single's release reaffirmed Ken Pitt's opinion of Angie as a 'predator,' and his suspicions that influence was irreversibly sliding away from him were verified in March, when the two arranged their marriage.

In subsequent years, as she dealt with their public and bitter divorce, Angie publicly doubted that David had ever loved her; indeed, some of her stories of their marriage decision describe him as asking, 'Can you bear the fact that I don't love you?' Angie has previously detailed how the pair realized they were in love during their Christmas 1969 separation, which Angie spent with her parents in Cyprus, eagerly awaiting letters. Following a ten-day mail strike, she received a card with the lines, 'We will marry, I promise, this year.'

The majority of David's own statements over the years reflect this grim image. At the time, David talked about their marriage as if it were a brand. He couldn't stomach thinking about Angie after their disastrously bad breakup. Those who were emotionally close to Angie and David in their early days, however, attribute their relationship to purer causes. Ava Cherry, who eventually became David's official girlfriend while he remained married to Angie - an official role equivalent to that of the King's mistress in the French Court - admits, 'I do think he felt love for her,' but adds, 'I'm giving her props she would never like me.' 'She was nurturing, and he needed that,' Ava continues, but more significantly, 'he liked the way she thought.'

Since the day they met, Angie and David's relationship had been open. Angie, she claims, foreshadowed this by arranging for them to spend the night before their March 20 wedding in bed with a lovely dark-haired actress they met through Calvin Lee. Ken Pitt had learned about the wedding from Peggy, who disliked Angie but decided to show up uninvited. John Cambridge was one of just three guys present, along with Roger the Roadie. Mick Ronson was not present, and Visconti was at work. David had asked Cambridge to be a witness, but when the registrar called out, Peggy, who was sat a few seats back, stepped up to sign the register. David shrugged his shoulders as he peered around at John. The wedding reception consisted of a beer at a neighboring pub.

When John Cambridge went to the Speakeasy with David and Angie a few days later, he was reminded of the Bowies' unconventional marriage. They were good friends by this point, and John had often heard David frolicking with other women at Haddon Hall, so he was surprised to find David dancing with "a bloke." 'But they only recently married!' John recalls thinking. Angie took John's hand and tried to pull him onto the dance floor as he watched. 'I turned around because that's how I was raised. I'm only nineteen years old and still very naive.' Years later, he wondered if frightening his young drummer and enjoying his reaction was part of David's attraction. And the intriguing notion that David was inspired by the nineteen-year-old's shame in 1972's 'John, I'm Only Dancing' lingers.

David's new wife's bravado would have a significant impact on David's career in several ways: one of her first acts was convincing Philips' Olav Wyper to advance £4000 to The Hype to fund living expenses, a PA system, and new tyres for the van, which had arrived at Haddon Hall with Rats roadie Roger, also known as Roger the Lodger.

The session would also come to an end. The session had been rescheduled at the last minute owing to a conflict with a live event in Scarborough, arranged by Ken Pitt. Ken had written a note to Haddon Hall confirming the live date, but the confusion heightened David's displeasure with the guy who'd been in charge of his career for the last three and a half years.

David called Olav Wyper's office in March to see if they might meet. 'He was plainly depressed - at times sobbing,' says Philips' CEO. 'He said he'd hit an impasse with Ken and that their relationship was impeding his career's progress. And he inquired, 'What do I believe, and how can I assist him?' In subsequent years, Wyper questioned if David's tears were staged; if so, they achieved the desired effect, causing him to sympathize with the sensitive vocalist. He had a duty to avoid a conflict of interest as the general manager of David's record label, but after asking David if he had a copy of his contract with Ken, which he didn't, he provided him the names of three firms that could advise him. The first person on the list was a pair of people Wyper knew well and who had recently chosen to start a business together. Laurence Myers and Tony Defries were their names.

Because of their position on the list provided by Olav Wyper, Defries and Myers were the first to be called. Several encounters took place during March, and Myers recalls being captivated by David Bowie. 'I liked him, and I thought David was a remarkable artist,' she says. However, it was Myers' business affairs manager, Defries, who recognized the potential of the young vocalist wishing to ditch his manager during their initial meetings. Tony Defries, according to Myers, had "the vision." His great gift was that he knew, far better than I did, what a star David was going to be.'

It's difficult to say how much Defries was sold on David's potential at their initial encounter, during which David spilled out his problems. However, David's predicament drew on Defries' problem-solving ability. He told David that he could get him out of Pitt's contract. Meanwhile, Pitt had no tangible evidence of David's displeasure until a meeting at his office on March 31, when David eventually informed him, 'Ken, I'd want to try managing myself.' The revelation came as little surprise to Pitt - 'I'd heard of at least one other management team who'd given David something' - but after committing to reduce the number of live performances and handing David a cheque for £200, the situation seemed to be settled, at least as far as Pitt was concerned. He continued to oversee arrangements, such as the next Mercury record sessions.

David's resolve was strengthened in other ways by his choice to get rid of Pitt. John Cambridge found a skipping bass drum section too difficult to play during a BBC radio session hosted by Bernie Andrews on March 25, a dry-run for the album sessions. David and Ronson were both patient and quiet. 'Of course you can do it, come on,' Ronson continued, and Cambridge finished the lesson. But John was gone within a fortnight. Mick 'Woody' Woodmansey took John's position in The Rats when Cambridge departed after being asked to rehearse on Easter Bank Holiday. Woodmansey, a more expansive drummer with a more serious, strong demeanor, suited the band's transition to a freer, more improvisational sound with his complicated rhythm patterns and flamboyant rolls. Visconti, on the other hand, appreciated Cambridge's strong, no-frills drumming and was startled to learn that it was Mick Ronson, not David, who had prompted the firing.

When it came to music, Ronson appeared to be just as objective as David Bowie. And when the album recording began on April 18 at Trident, it was the guitarist who took command of the sessions, approaching recording with the same determination with which he'd mastered the guitar. Visconti, who had far more studio expertise than Ronson, recalls affectionately, 'It was Mick who was our guru - anything he instructed us to do, we'd do.' Ronson was in charge of the arrangements, convincing Visconti to use a Gibson short-scale bass for a more fluid guitar-like sound, writing down synthesizer lines for Ralph Mace, and even duetted on recorder with Visconti. In sharp contrast to Bowie, who was 'just plain tough to nail down' at times, Mick was everywhere, dominating the texture and feel of the album titled The Man Who Sold the World.

David had been remarkably unassertive on his first Mercury album; this time, he seemed more confident, but still surprisingly casual, leaving enormous amounts of work to Ronson and Visconti, who says, 'As a novice producer, I just couldn't understand why David wouldn't want to be in the studio every minute with us.' In recent years, David has sounded irritated by Visconti's remarks, which highlight his own, dominant position in the writing: 'Who else writes chord sequences like that?' However, Ken Scott, the session's engineer, recalls Ronson and Visconti controlling every element of a record in which Bowie was mostly absent. 'Tony and Mick took over. I'm not sure how much of it was David refusing to participate and how much was Tony taking over. But I believe Tony's ideas were more prominent on the CD than David's.'

Visconti's dissatisfaction with Bowie stemmed more from 'they and us' divisions than from musical differences. David's crush on Angie was natural, but what was more galling was that 'David was the only one of us who had money in the bank, from "Space Oddity," while we were living on nothing.' These unusual, sometimes pleasurable, but frequently dysfunctional conditions provided the setting for Bowie's first great, albeit flawed, album. There had been little emotional commitment in his prior works: 'Space Oddity' was simply estrangement, and even in a nice, personal song like 'Letter to Hermione,' he sounded dissatisfied rather than distraught. However, he was able to surf the wave of noise created by Ronson and Visconti for this record, using them as a vehicle to enhance his own feelings.

The recording of The Man Who Sold the World captures a dilemma that would recur throughout David Bowie's career: how much of his work was his own, and how much was the work of his subordinates? This reliance on his sidemen was a fault, according to opponents, who used reasons similar to those used to criticize modern artists like Andy Warhol, who simply planned out themes and let colleagues like Gerard Malanga to execute their screen prints or movies.

Visconti's thoughts on the matter are complicated, but he summarizes them by saying, 'With a smile on my face, I have to say that Mick and I couldn't have written such a wonderful album with anyone else.' The message appears to be straightforward: the album is a Ronson and Visconti album with David Bowie, rather than a David Bowie album with Ronson and Visconti. However, ownership of the album is complicated because Bowie sparked creativity in both Ronson and Visconti that might otherwise have lain dormant. David's songwriting in his Lower Third days was mostly straight thievery. The moral position was more complicated in this case. Visconti and Ronson's work as Ronno were completely forgettable without Bowie. Can you truly steal' something that would not exist without you?

The complex, emotional environment that gave birth to The Man Who Sold the World became even murkier when, halfway through the sessions, David wrote to Ken, informing him that he no longer considered him his manager and asking him - in misunderstood legal jargon - to confirm his intention to cease acting as such within seven days. He and Tony Defries were at Pitt's Manchester Street office a week later. Defries was low-key but did all of the talking; as was his wont, he faced the situation head-on but deferred the difficult specifics until later - in this case, compensating Pitt for the money he'd spent on David.

The meeting was terrible for Pitt. The warning signs were evident in retrospect, but David's desertion was a brutal, unexpected blow. All those who knew him at the time, including Wyper, recall him as visibly traumatized - but also touchingly concerned about David's career. Today, Pitt recounts a slew of arrangements he had planned for Bowie, including a trip to New York on a Cunard liner using all of his Warhol connections, all of which may have helped the singer get out of the career rut he was in. When asked if he was too gentlemanly for the music industry, Pitt's visage darkens before he says, 'Perhaps I wasn't assertive enough. But, my God, I reached into my pocket and spent the money on David, which they weren't doing at the time.'

Defries performed a fatherly, consultative role in the early post-Pitt days, mostly talking about problem solving. He wasn't very pushy at first, but he was a skilled name-dropper who seemed to have a special affinity for the artistic temperament. He highlighted how he would safeguard the valuable objects they made, their intellectual property rights, as if it were a sacred vocation, and how he was at the forefront of such a movement, freeing artists from the grips of incompetent record labels.

The Man Who Sold the World was finished on May 22, but as the tapes were handed over to Philips, the record business was embroiled in complications that seemed to vindicate Tony Defries' skepticism about record labels. In the autumn of 1970, he learned that his label champion, Olav Wyper, was being fired. David had to deal with being an orphan artist.

Wyper's departure was quickly followed by the disappearances of Tony Visconti and Mick Ronson. David Bowie's defection would become a well-known staging point in his career. Another disadvantage is opaque in comparison. By the end of the year, the new manager who had vowed to advocate David Bowie had also vanished. David Bowie would be most alone just as he'd proved how much he needed followers to help him realize his goal.

Part Two:
Things That Are Hollow

Chapter 4: It is not free to change.

As 1973 came to a close, David Bowie in London and Tony Defries in New York reflected on their accomplishments. They'd finally outwitted the system. But neither of them could wait to get started.
Defries, who detested old-school, bloated record business management, was erecting an overstaffed empire that mimicked the system he despised. And David, who had written a manifesto establishing himself as a new species of human, couldn't wait to meet the previous generation of rock stars. They were each aware of the contradictions in the other's perspective, but not in their own. 'They were a fairly great partnership up to that moment,' says Tony Zanetta, who admired – perhaps revered – both men. 'However, once everything came to a halt and they could enjoy the rewards of their achievement, cracks began to develop.'

Those flaws would have no effect on Defries' calm sense of self-worth; David Bowie, on the other hand, could not stand to think about them, burying his concerns so deeply that the ultimate crisis would be completely heartbreaking.

Meanwhile, David is looking for role models. Iggy and Lou were no longer enough for him; instead, he shifted his attention to their apparent polar opposite, Mick Jagger. Mick was always a rival, not an idol. David, who was out to knock Jagger off his pedestal, was also obsessed with him. He and Ava enjoyed several dinners with Mick and Bianca, conversing volubly, with the duo even noodling on a tune together one night, which became the Astronettes song 'Having a Good Time'. But neither could shake their sleek, polished reputations. 'It was polite and smart, but they didn't breach a boundary,' Cherry says. Angie Bowie later stated how she caught Bowie and Mick in bed together, which is absurd to anyone who has seen the two together. Each guy was guarded, and even twenty years later would be almost obsessively aware of his relative standing; the idea of one being entirely open with the other, let alone being 'a bottom' was unfathomable. The two personalities appeared similar to Ava; bright, competitive, with a similar dry or camp humor, yet they were extremely different. David was usually engrossed in some obsession or excitement. Mick was not one of them. 'He was never under the influence of anything,' says Maggie Abbott, who eventually became Mick and David's movie agent. 'He was always completely in command. He was the stereotypical Leo, far more disciplined than David. He'd never be duped by anything.'

Despite his actions, David was terrified by his adversary, who was an old hand at dealing with pretenders to his kingdom. From enlisting the coolest African-American lovers, such as Marsha Hunt, to penning songs in a Burroughsian cut-up style, as Mick had done for Exile on Main Street in 1971, Jagger had paved the way for many of David's interests. But it wasn't until a Rolling Stones gig in Newcastle that spring that Bowie realized he could beat the Stones' frontman. He was standing in the wings with confidant Scott Richardson, telling him about the time he offered to carry Brian Jones' guitar and was told to piss off. The pair became aware that Jagger was staring at them from center stage. They noticed hundreds of fans ignoring the band and craning their necks to glimpse the carrot-haired presence at the side of the stage.

As was his custom, David attacked the issue of measuring up to Jagger by entering his domain and liberally taking from him. This, combined with Keith Harwood, the Stones' favorite engineer at the time, influenced his choice of Olympic as his working studio. While the lyrical foundation of David's second album was a reworking of his 1984 concept, with its chaotic, dystopian edge heightened by his use of Burroughs' cut-up technique, the musical blueprint was unabashedly based on The Rolling Stones.

'Rebel Rebel,' a beautifully simple tune that signaled Bowie's farewell to the Ziggy era, would go on to become one of his best-known hits. Parker was surprised a few years later when he discovered that, in addition to composing the riff, Bowie was credited in the album notes with playing the guitar on the finished version. Because of the fluctuating tempo and audio spill between the studio microphones, even the most accomplished guitarist would struggle to replace Parker's work. 'I can tell my own playing and sound,' Parker says, 'and I know it's me.'

The emphasis on David's job as guitarist seems geared to demonstrate to Mick Ronson, whose solo career was briefly booming, how well David could survive without him. 'It's ridiculous... 'I'm not sure why it would matter so much,' says Parker, who has previously spoken with both Ronson and Bowie. The uncertainty over the credits was all the more useless, considering the fantastic job David did of playing guitar on the remaining songs, notably the title track - which with its cowbell and loose backing vocals mirrored 'Honky Tonk Women' - and the jagged, New Wave-ish guitar on 'Candidate'.

Look closer, and the pettiness was more easily comprehended, because in the latter months of 1973, David's world was collapsing around him. He was pretty upbeat at the start of the sessions, energized by the challenge of playing the electric guitar and enjoying the camaraderie of the studio, dropping in on Mott guitarist Mick Ralph's new band, Bad Company, who were mixing at Olympic. That friendship was shattered, however, when Bowie was barred from the studio following an argument; by the end of the sessions, there was precious little good will left.

David's musical isolation, his reliance on session men - yes-men, actually - had an advantage in that it brought a fresh intensity to his work. Outside the studio, though, his solitude was toxic, exacerbated by the increasing instability and backbiting within MainMan. MainMan's cashflow troubles worsened dramatically after Tony Defries left for New York. Corinne Schwab, one of the company's latest hires, did a spectacular job regulating the company's UK finances, but even she couldn't talk the Château D'Hérouville out of banning all MainMan acts in a disagreement over unpaid costs.

As David's suspicions rose that Tony Defries, the father figure who controlled so much of his life, was presiding over a financial disaster, he discovered the ideal psychological crutch, one that had contributed to the Rolling Stones' aura of glitter and decadence: cocaine.

Cocaine's peak coincided with the destruction of the last vestiges of the 'we' decade and the emergence of the me' decade. Cocaine, which was regarded to be a benign, non-addictive narcotic at the time - 'We thought it helped us be smarter and more creative,' explains MainMan's Tony Zanetta - would wreck the psyche of a generation of artists. Its victims included New Stones guitarist Ron Wood and Iggy; Iggy was eventually committed to a mental institution as a result. Keith Christmas, a member of the upbeat, cooperative Beckenham environment, witnessed the drug's effects on David and many others and shudders as he recalls them. 'It's a horrible drug. It causes people to act like utter jerks. Because it removes a lot of our anxious emotional desire not to upset other people, it allows you to feel like you can upset anybody the fuck you want. People would be having a nice time at a party then someone mentioned coke, and the entire atmosphere would shift. "Get some coke in, get some lines in," was all anyone could say. Its compulsive nature is terrifying.'

Despite being a compulsive coffee and cigarette smoker, David had been practically saintly in his abstinence from other substances. 'It was so strange,' Tony Zanetta remembers, 'he didn't smoke weed, he just drank a couple of glasses of white wine. It happened so quickly - cocaine was absolutely something he absorbed into what it meant to be a rock star.'

Ava Cherry recalls David's 'occasional toot' as coinciding with the seeming financial catastrophe. 'He was in a bad mood... stating these people had stolen all my money. And [cocaine] would be a crutch at first: "It calms me down." Angie, too, believes David's cocaine addiction began during these weeks. 'It's what they did to him, my baby,' she laments in a rare display of tenderness, blaming the drug for their marriage's demise.

David's mental state would undoubtedly have an impact on his music. Although some of Diamond Dogs' songs were languid and beautiful - 'Sweet Thing/Candidate', for example - the recording had an obsessive air to it, with jagged guitars and saxophones piled ominously on top of one other. The poetic imagery was also grim, with stories of the Diamond Dogs based on Haywood Jones' descriptions of Dickensian London, when orphan children filled the rooftops of London rookeries. The resulting intensity constituted a significant aural and spiritual break from the optimism of his three Spiders albums. This new territory was fertile and marked a progression in David's work, but there was a sacrifice as well. in the obsessive focus on sound, texture, and an almost physical heaviness, the deftness of Hunky Dory and Ziggy Stardust - with their swooping melodies and restlessly mobile chord sequences - had vanished.

Bolder agreed and arrived at Barnes to find Bowie, Mike Garson, and drummer Tony Newman working on an acoustic song. Sitting in the studio with Bowie but no Spiders was an unsettling experience. Before running tape, the quartet practiced the song multiple times. 'But it was a nothing tune,' Bolder explains, 'and it definitely got dumped afterwards.' After the take, Bolder put his bass guitar away while Bowie sat with his back to him.

'I'm gone now, Dave, I'll see you later,' Bolder said. Bowie remained silent. Bolder said it again. 'Then I'm leaving. See you later! Bye.' Bowie ignored him once more. In silence, the ex-Spider strolled out of the studio, taking one last glance at Bowie's back, silhouetted against the control-room glass. It was their final time sharing a studio.

Bowie's teenage friend Wayne Bardell ran into him in Tramp's nightclub around the same time. He walked over to him, overjoyed to see his pal, with whom he'd last spoken during the first Ziggy tour.
'How are you doing?'
'Hi. 'Who are you?' David inquired.
'That hurt,' says Bardell, who sat in on the recording of 'Pity the Fool' and had seen David on a regular basis for the previous nine years. 'I was also using cocaine... However, this did not prevent me from knowing others. This was freezing. Calculated.'

The freezing out of those who had known him since his days as a struggling artist was common in the 1970s - Marc Bolan demonstrated a nastier version of the tendency, aided once again by cocaine usage. David wasn't mean; he just cut them off brutally. After hearing from Tony Visconti that the home studio he was building was lacking in furniture, he sent around a Conran Shop van packed with office chairs, as well as a dining suite and crockery - later, they'd mix the majority of the Diamond Dogs tracks there.

David's persona has always had a childlike quality to it - that clear-eyed honesty was an inherent part of his attraction. However, once twisted by the flattery of junior MainMan personnel, the frequent attentions of chefs or maids, and the other corrosive impacts of stardom, that childishness was no longer so endearing. As Ava Cherry recalls, "children believe the entire world revolves around them." Everyone pushed David to think in this manner.' Certain pals, most notably Ron Wood, whom David knew from his Marquee days, would learn to handle David's moods. David reconnected with the guitarist after the Diamond Dogs recordings were relocated to Hilversum, the Netherlands, where the Stones were also working. The two connected over their shared love of Peter Cook and Dudley Moore, memorizing and imitating their conversations. 'Ronny was extremely good at making you feel like you were having fun,' Ava Cherry remembers, 'and I always felt fantastic when Ronny came around. Because David was never furious; he was always laughing.'

During the same time frame, David developed a deeper, more lasting relationship. Hugh Attwooll employed Corinne 'Coco' Schwab in the summer of 1973. The UK office manager of MainMan thought she was well educated, clever, and capable. He quickly realized she was "smarter than me, for sure." I recruited her, and within a month, I was gone, and she had taken over my job.' By the autumn of 1973, Corinne was the sole person keeping the MainMan UK office afloat, since the financial situation had become "intolerable," according to Tony Zanetta: "She was abandoned in the English office, Defries refused to pay almost any bills, David was spending wildly." She has earned her place.'

Defries admired Coco's old-school efficiency, her mastery of languages, and her cosmopolitan background; born on her mother's shopping trip to Bloomingdales in New York, she told her friends, she had been educated in America, Europe, and Kashmir. Defries initially supported her rising in order to lessen Angie's power. Coco had become David's personal assistant by the autumn of 1973 (a role Suzi Fussey turned down in order to marry Mick Ronson) and was put on the top floor of Oakley Street, where she controlled access to David.

Corinne would become a pivotal figure in David's life: clever, thin, and funny, she appeared nearly anonymous in other ways. This contributed to her allure and efficacy. She looked content to commit herself entirely to David, with no agenda of her own to impose on him. Many years later, in his song devoted to Coco, 'Never Let Me Down,' David would sing of "your soothing hand that turned me round." The song refers to her as a lover, but in reality she served as a combination mother, sister, lover, and - most importantly - all-purpose intellectual confidante, similar to the paid companions employed by cultured ladies of a certain age. 'David liked her because she was intellectual and they could have wonderful talks,' recalls Ava Cherry, adding that Corinne was 'in love with [David] from day one'. David relished Corinne's unwavering devotion to his cause, and would periodically mock Ava with anecdotes about how indispensable she'd become. In February, Ava was moved over to New York, purportedly to connect up with Tony Defries and organize David's move to the city, but Cherry soon determined that Schwab 'systematically did nothing except try and get me out'.

David turned to another exotic species in Ava's absence: Amanda Lear. Lear, a former muse of Bryan Ferry and a friend of Salvador Dali, helped David celebrate his 27th birthday by taking him to watch Fritz Lang's 1926 classic Metropolis. In the weeks leading up to his departure for America, David immersed himself in Lang's work, which, coupled with the staging he'd originally intended for Arnold Corns, formed the foundation of the visuals for his next American tour. He'd wanted to offer his acts as a three-dimensional extravaganza since 1971. Now he was planning a fresh, grandiose vision with no concessions.

On April 1, 1974, David landed in New York after sailing the Atlantic with Geoff MacCormack on the SS France. The one-way trip was rife with symbolism, both positive and negative; David planned to base himself in America, a country he'd long wished to visit, soak up its aura, and dominate it. And he needed Tony Defries to help him solve his problems.

The relocation to New York was ideal for soaking up the atmosphere. Bowie utilized Ava Cherry as his guide to the soul scene after relocating into the Sherry Netherland Hotel near Central Park. Ava suggested they check out Harlem's Apollo Theater, where it turned out there was a show on the 26th topped by Richard Pryor, featuring The Main Ingredient: one of RCA's few cool bands, the Harlem outfit had changed line-up in 1972, recruiting new singer, Cuba Gooding Sr, and scored a huge soul smash with 'Everybody Plays the Fool'. The audience at the Apollo was predominantly black, with the red-haired, pasty-faced Bowie standing out like a white cat in a coal scuttle. 'He loved it,' Ava says. 'He lapped it all in.'

Norman Fisher, a stockbroker turned art collector noted for the lavish parties he'd host in his little Downtown apartment, was another joyous source of Americana to be discovered in 1974. David recalls them as "the most diverse soirees in all of New York." People from all walks of the avant-garde would congregate there - Norman was a magnet.' Fisher introduced David to some of the most brilliantly varied art and music: Florence Jenkins, the famously terrible opera singer who drew big audiences in the 1920s with her absurd costumes and atonal performances, was one example. Norman not only provided nice company but also cocaine to his social group. 'But he didn't want to,' Ava explains. 'Norman just wanted to hang out with folks and be buddies.'

Fisher was a close friend of David's for many years, and she embodied the splendor of New York. However, in his capacity as David's supplier, he unknowingly aided in a deep shift. 'I met David at the NBC Special [in October 1973] and noticed no drug problem,' Tony Zanetta adds. 'Then, in April 1974, it was there: full-blown.'

David's obviously altered state would be just another element in his relationship with Tony Defries failing. Moving closer to Defries was supposed to energize their relationship, but instead it strained it. Diamond Dogs received negative reviews upon its release in April

1974, yet it went on to become David's best-selling album in the United States, peaking at number five. Defries, on the other hand, favored more showbiz themes, such as Ziggy Stardust and the brief songs contained inside it. Furthermore, he disapproved of David's budding preparations for his next, extravagant tour.

This was typical of a man in charge of a company that now employed twenty-five full-time employees and had its own travel agency, as well as a TV, radio, and movie production company. It was especially galling to David because Defries was often bragging about his own generosity, such as his idea to fulfill his employees' "ultimate fantasy." (Leee Childers had his teeth cleaned; Cherry Vanilla used her bonus to get a breast job.)

Defries' generosity, as usual, did not extend to David's musicians. David had planned a recording session with Lulu in his first weeks in New York, with the assistance of Main Ingredient founder Tony Silvester. Carlos Alomar, Silvester's new guitarist, was proposed. Carlos Alomar, a former member of the Apollo house band and a session regular for everyone from Peter, Paul, and Mary to Roy Ayers, arrived at RCA studios and was impressed by Bowie's red hair and "mousey skin." It was incredibly translucent. And the black under his eyes seemed a little frightening.' Following the session, Alomar invited David to his Queens home for a nice lunch and was surprised when the singer showed up, spending the evening talking about soul albums and grilling Alomar on his work with Chuck Berry and James Brown. 'He's always astonished me in that sense - he's always willing to dive right in.'

That evening, David invited Carlos to join him on his upcoming tour, and Carlos, excited by the idea of moving behind 'the chitlin' mindset,as typified by famously cheapskate bosses like James Brown or Chuck Berry, found himself a white manager to negotiate the arrangement. Only then did Carlos realize that MainMan would only pay half of his weekly $800 from The Main Ingredient. Regrettably, he returned to his session work, leaving David to locate some less expensive musicians.

In his search for a new band, David contacted Keith Christmas, who had previously played acoustic guitar on the Space Oddity record. Christmas, a brilliant musician with a distinct English folk sound, seemed out of place in Bowie's new surroundings. When he arrived in New York, he was greeted by "a punch of pretentious fucking posers, so full of themselves with their dyed white hair and shaved heads." It had a decidedly sleazy and unpleasant vibe to it.'

Christmas was an acoustic guitarist, and his electric performance was barely acceptable, but the surroundings were strange: the enormous RCA studios on the Avenue of the Americas, deserted save for Bowie, Christmas, and an engineer running tape. When David needed a 'toot,' he would call down the corridor to Christmas, who would huddle together secretly in the bathrooms. 'So this is all a bit paranoid. I'll never forget how he was carving out lines with this double-sided razor blade. When he placed his finger in a small bindle of coke and held it up to my nose, I noticed how much his hand was shaking, which meant, 'I want this drug so badly that I'm willing to risk serious personal injury for it.'

The encounter was upsetting. Despite the paranoid, frightening exterior, Christmas believes this is the same person he knew in 1969. 'David truly appeared to be entirely at ease. In terms of who he was as a person, it was a continuation of the Art Lab days; the people had changed, and the drugs had maybe changed. However, the actual individual may not have changed at all.' David asked Christmas to embrace his hippie trip in Beckenham, just as he asked Bob Grace to join the sexually ambiguous Sombrero scene. The covert ritual of sniffing cocaine in a toilet was a new trip for a new identity, but it was not one he would readily abandon.

Within a few days of being in New York, David contacted an old friend of Ossie Clark's, Michael Kamen - another creative, transplanted Brit with a serious cocaine problem with whom David hung out. Kamen led a rock 'n' roll band with saxophonist David Sanborn and had lately added guitarist Earl Slick, but he was also a formidable classical pianist. Kamen had recently written the music for a ballet based on the biography of Auguste Rodin, and Bowie and MacCormack were captivated by the New York premiere. David's ideas on dance and staging were reflected by Kamen's cross-cultural connections, and the composer was hired as musical director.

The extravagant staging for David's new show, as original as it appeared, was actually based on ideas he'd been playing with since May of 1971. When imagining how to display Arnold Corns, he pictured the band playing in an open-sided boxing ring surrounded by massive pillars each supporting a single white spot: 'It has to be remorseless,' he explained to a puzzled Freddie Buretti. 'I don't want any colors; I want everything to be stark.' Later, his Rainbow show plans were limited by budget and time; now, he robbed MainMan's rapidly depleting funds to realize his fantasies. Hunger City, a decaying future metropolis with thirty-foot-high buildings, was portrayed by a massive stage background, which was supplemented by a motorized bridge, a remote-control mirrored module, and a cherry-picker in which David would descend from the heavens. Bowie would perform in the boxing ring for 'Rebel Rebel,' wearing huge leather boxing gloves and a mask reminiscent of the mime he'd filmed for Ken Pitt.

The transformation of David himself was far more startling for many admirers than the new, mechanized backdrop. He had come in New York with his spiky carrot-top largely intact; now it had been replaced by a forties-style 'do, with parting and floppy fringe, and the Yamamoto ensembles had been replaced by a double-breasted suit with high-waisted pants, a skinny jumper, and braces. The style was clearly influenced by 1940s Harlem, as well as another hero, Frank Sinatra. However, David's consciously 'cool' image was inspired by someone much closer to home: Roxy Music's Bryan Ferry, whose stage movements he closely studied; David practiced Bryan's gestures, including a distinctive movement made by the Roxy singer with his index finger, and incorporated the wiggle into his own repertoire of stage mannerisms.

The sight of goggle-eyed Ziggy clones aghast at David's new earthly manifestation, and overwhelmed by the visual smorgasbord - which included loose street' dancing choreographed by Toni Basil - when the tour opened in Canada on 14 June, less than a year after Bowie's Retirement', was a vindication of the weeks of preparation. However, the equipment was in disarray, putting David in continual danger of electrocution. The set blended conservatism - an emphasis on the hits, and some self-consciously bombastic arrangements - with subtlety and risk; 'The Jean Genie's' verse was turned into an urban rap, like Lou's 'Walk on the Wild Side', while The Ohio Players' 'Here Today and Gone Tomorrow', delivered at later shows, was delivered straight, showcasing the soul pipes David had been developing ever since 'Pity the Fool'. The rhythms were slick and relentless, thanks to old-school session hands Herbie Flower and Tony Newman; the night 'rocked real hard,' as Detroiter Robert Matheu, a veteran of shows by the MC5 and Stooges, recalls.

Despite this, the initial series of shows, the result of such tremendous labor and obsessiveness, would become known as a beacon of pessimism due to the ill-will surrounding the recording of the Philadelphia shows between July 8 and 12. The players that came at the venue and found extra microphones were the first sign that MainMan intended to release an album of the night's performance without paying any extra expenses, according to bassist Herbie Flowers. Earl Slick, a guitarist, recalls benefiting from Flowers' steadfast performance as a shop steward during a stand-up row between MainMan and the musicians. Flowers maintains that the controversy was "blown out of proportion." We inquired, "Do we get any money?" and were told that we would be paid at the American Musicians' Union rate.' Only a smirk remained in his remark on the tour's staging. 'I've always liked opera,' he says. 'But it was pantomime,' she says.

John Peel, David's former hero, was less complimentary of David's mundane cover of "Knock on Wood," which preceded the live album in September, calling it "lazy, arrogant, and impertinent." The same might be said of the David Live CD, which was released in October: despite many inventive moments, the performances were grandiose, feeling more like the output of a corporate behemoth than a vocalist. Nonetheless, it was one of David's most successful US releases to date, landing at number eight; in the UK, the Bay City Rollers maintained the top spot. Many early Bowie supporters, those who initially championed Bowie in the press or saw him at little venues like Friars Aylesbury, considered it as filler, a sign of a creative drought. However, after a few months, they would be compelled to reconsider.

David had embarked on an obsessive exploration of cutting edge R&B since seeing The Main Ingredient in April, which soon extended beyond the obligatory Aretha Franklin to boxes of soul vinyl obtained for him by LA writer Harvey Kubernick, including Philly International singles by Harold Melvin and the Bluenotes and Patti Labelle, and MFSB, the Philly soul band who recorded the Soul Train theme tune. David watched the popular music show every week, generally in a party setting with fellow soul fans like Geoff MacCormack. David was drawn to Ava Cherry in part because she embodied US soul culture. He pumped her for information, like he did so many of his confidantes, all of which filtered into his life and business. 'My father was a musician in the 1940s [in Chicago] - black folks used to wear loose pants called gousters. "My father has a couple of pairs of ties and suits," I once told David. "Really?" he exclaimed. Where? "Could you bring some?" So I brought over a couple of my father's silk ties and a pair of gouster pants with suspenders [braces].'

Many of David's prior creative swerves had required months of planning; manifestos drafted at Haddon Hall, musicians flown in from as far away as Hull. Things could move faster in America. The new lineup of musicians was assembled in a single phone call. A pair of pants served as the foundation for the new appearance. David dressed up in his gouster suit, complete with silk ties and suspenders, and informed his lover, 'I'm going to record a session right now.'

Chapter 5: Make me cry and break down

During a brief layover in New York, David called Carlos Alomar, the guitarist he'd met in Queens but couldn't recruit due to MainMan's stinginess. 'Look, Carlos,' he said, 'I'm going to be in Philadelphia, to Sigma Sound.' He used persuasion skills gained over years of dealing with musicians. 'I know you just got done working there, but I really need you to come down.' The guitarist liked David's charisma, but he didn't need much convincing to leave the chitlin' circuit after he'd established David would match his current wage.

The musical shift signaled by 'Young Americans' is unmistakable, but the lyrics are just as representative of his magpie tendencies. 'Young Americans,' a complete departure from Diamond Dogs' shattered images, is observational - musical reportage with dialogue: 'They drove in close below the bridge. He sets her down, frowns, and says, "Gee, my life's a funny thing"... The music was funky, but the lyrical style was a dead ringer for Bruce Springsteen, whom David and Geoff had seen at Max's. To add to the homage, David recorded a cover of Bruce's 'It's Hard to Be a Saint in the City,' which he delivered in his new baritone croon, a combination between Elvis, Sinatra, and Bryan Ferry. During the session, Tony Visconti discovered Bruce lived nearby - in a caravan, he recalls - and invited him to the studio. Bruce was perplexed, perplexed that this English glam artist was covering one of his songs and lavishly complimenting him; eventually, David's zeal won him over, and they talked about music late into the night.

The aura of intensity around the Sigma meetings was a stark contrast to David's chaotic personal life. Ava, his partner, had inspired his work in the city, although he'd frequently vanish during the recordings, like a cat on the prowl. 'I knew the party was going on somewhere else,' Cherry says of his late-night exploits. When Angie arrived in Philadelphia, she heard Ava was on the scene and dashed towards a hotel window, threatening to hurl herself out.

Angie's behavior was all the more outrageous because she was one of the few people who didn't drink or do drugs at the time. David and Angie were trapped in a peculiar loop in which David would decide he needed her and call her up; Angie would arrive, only to be ignored, resulting in a crisis. 'It was a really strange relationship, extremely strange to be around,' Zanetta concluded, realizing over these weeks that David was thinking about ultimately getting rid of Angie. The timing was critical because it came just a few days after David's belated realization of his relationship with MainMan.

The harrowing chat took place at the end of July in a New York hotel. Bowie, like Zanetta, was stoned out of his mind when he poured out his woes: 'Did I work this hard, to have nothing?' When the two were discussing the money that was pouring out of MainMan, Zanetta realized that David believed he controlled half of the company. 'It was strange,' Zanetta admits. 'He didn't realize he didn't own [half of] MainMan. We sat there, going through what had gone wrong and attempting to keep everything together. I admired both David and Tony, so this was more than painful - it was as if the world had ended.'

As traumatic as the situation was for Zanetta, it was even worse for David. He'd simply assumed he controlled his own firm and his own music; the fact, as outlined by Zanetta, was so drastically different that he seemed unable to comprehend it. Zanetta attempted to explain to him that he held half of his own revenue, less expenses, but had no ownership in the other MainMan businesses. If David wanted to guarantee he had received what he was entitled to, the obvious next step was to employ an accountant and check over the accounts, where every penny of expenditure was documented. But David was uninterested in analyzing his situation. Defries had conjured up a mystical aura, a cocoon in which David might work. The magical bubble had now popped. David made no effort to research his contract with MainMan in the following weeks; he was only interested in canceling it. 'Their relationship was coming to an end,' says Zanetta, their conflicted go-between. 'Money was a factor. Defries' megalomania played a role. They were both megalomaniacs, in truth.

'Tony was a total father figure,' Ava Cherry adds. 'David would do anything," Tony remarked, listening to his every word. He was simply... terrified when he learned about the money.'

The repercussions of David's pact with MainMan were complicated; there were benefits to the way David's contract was put up, as it offered him authority over his masters - as long as he stayed with MainMan. Defries claims that MainMan's unique position as owner of David's master recordings increased his royalties from the industry normal 10% to 16%, a cut that was extraordinarily generous in the early 1970s. But one critical component of their relationship is unarguable. David thought he was a partner in MainMan, but he was actually an employee. His inability to even examine his own rank demonstrated astounding naiveté.

David's self-esteem suffered greatly as a result of this finding. His father figure, in his opinion, had betrayed him. Ava Cherry and Coco consoled him during his frantic weeping fits whenever he thought about his predicament, but most of the time, his troubles were too grim to comprehend. Instead, David focused on Angie, realizing he couldn't take her outbursts any longer. He would continue to play his public role with his wife for months to come, maintaining the image that, as Scott Richardson puts it, "had made the world fall in love with them," but David's emotional distance from Angie was part of his alienation from MainMan. Angie had shaped MainMan's image more than David had; it was she who had built the company's cradle at Haddon Hall, who had formed the bond with the Pork team. 'MainMan had been constructed in Angie's image,' says Leee Childers. Both were now burdens for David. But, for the time being, he would preserve his silence while he figured out how to let himself go.

The summer of 1974 was mild and pleasant, and when David resumed his tour with Carlos Alomar, Ava Cherry, and the majority of the Sigma team, his personal traumas were temporarily forgotten in the exhilaration of creation. For the time being, David informed Defries, through Tony Zanetta, that he was creating a new stripped-down performance in which he would abandon the Hunger City set and perform against a white backdrop. Defries pretended to be unconcerned when he learned that the $400,000 development was doomed.

David's claim to bona fide superstar status was set out convincingly over seven nights at Hollywood's Universal Amphitheatre. His previous retirement' appeared to have simply added to his unpredictability and glamor. The Hollywood nobility showed up; Diana Ross, dressed in a silver gown, as did her fellow Motown singers The Jackson Five.

Marc Bolan was another of the conquering hero's entourage. He had slammed David in print earlier that year, dismissing his American triumph as a marketing gimmick. Now, chubby and uncomfortable, he paid his respects to the guy who had so frequently praised him. 'David was definitely at a high moment, and Marc was obviously at a bad point,' adds Zanetta, who sat with them at the Beverly Wilshire hotel. 'But David was quite courteous and did not gloat at all.' Later that year, Marc told Melody Maker about directing David in his first film. Marc's swagger appeared terribly sad by then, with David being courted by Hollywood's biggest stars. Iggy Pop ultimately made an appearance as well. Following a legendarily catastrophic last tour, Iggy had finally left from The Stooges after his separation with MainMan and well-publicized attacks on 'that fuckin' carrot-top' for destroying his Raw Power album. His previous public appearance had been a pitiful shambles at Rodney's English Disco, culminating in him cutting his chest with a blunt steak knife. Iggy, who is now derided in Hollywood as a trashy drug user, missed David's gig after being bashed up in the parking lot by a gang of surfers. He returned later to scavenge food.

Burying himself in musical preparations throughout the LA gigs, David seemed truly delighted; over several nights he taught Ava Cherry, ready for her solo song, which was Luther Vandross's 'Maybe It's Love'. He was the ideal tutor, rehearsing with her and encouraging her. 'He guided me through the entire thing, the movement, the way I'd take the stage. It was fantastic because he was so nurturing.'

David had even acted courteous and welcoming when a young BBC director, Alan Yentob, emerged in Hollywood, explaining that Tony Defries had consented to allow him access in a sudden slip. David agreed to an interview after hearing Yentob's explanation of the documentary's concept - that it would be a study of a significant, serious artist in his new, American setting.

During his time in Hollywood, David was courted by the UK's most glamorous cinematic icon: Elizabeth Taylor. Terry O'Neill, who photographed David for the Diamond Dogs sleeve, invited David to a shoot at filmmaker George Cukor's residence, for which David came "two hours late - disheveled and out of it." Liz was irritated and on the edge of leaving, but we persuaded her to stay.' Liz's dislike for David was outweighed by her desire for attention. Taylor, who had been a major celebrity in the 1960s, had done less well in the 1970s and was keen to be connected with Bowie: O'Neill's photographs showed the two frolicking like teenagers, Liz embracing David and holding his cigarette suggestively.

Within a few days, she was paying high-profile visits to David's rehearsals and floating the idea in the press that David would feature in The Blue Bird, a remake of Maurice Tourneur's 1918 film. Her endorsement of David as an upcoming celebrity was made official at a Ricci Martin - Dean's son - party in Beverly Hills, where they sat close to each other, softly conversing.

David, whom Farren knew from his Lindsay Kemp days, appeared lost and 'lonely' when he wasn't on stage. He mostly went around in an overcoat, hood up, nose dripping, twitchingly refusing any efforts at conversation. He seemed afraid when anyone entered the lift with him. Many outsiders recall a cutthroat, paranoid atmosphere, with separate cliques attempting to coax others back to their room 'for some blow,' each accusing the others of being drug addicts, if not outright stealing money. But David was always in command onstage, and the backstage tension gave the music an edge. 'David had people playing against each other on stage to improve them,' Ava Cherry adds, 'like the James Brown thing, always that pressure of, You're in, You're out. It was excellent at moments. Because we were opposites, me and Diane [Sumler] would fight harder to outperform each other.

The autumn and winter of 1974 were highlighted by a cocaine blitz, during which David memorably described himself as being "out of my gourd." Even strangers, while concerned by David's physical decline, were persuaded that this was only a phase that would pass. 'He's such a survivor,' says Mick Farren, 'besides we weren't all dying back then.' Farren claims that it was only in retrospect that he realized the psychological burdens David had taken on. 'It's like what John Lennon said about Elvis: "I don't know how he did it, 'cos there were four of us and it nearly killed us." Of course, there were only two Davids.'

David's appearance on The Dick Cavett Show during the New York concerts on November 2, 1974, was the pinnacle of his 'out of my gourd' moment, and the perfect distillation of the tour's prickly, paranoid spirit. Sniffing loudly and shifting his gaze from side to side, David bares his teeth several times in a grimace reminiscent of the skeleton masks that had terrified him in Boston. Cavett cites dark magic and how some folks indicated they're terrified to sit and talk to you,' as if in response. David's major reaction is to play with his cane incessantly, and Cavett appears concerned for a brief period, as if his guest is drawing a pentagram on the studio floor. He manages to simulate a regular human being at times - a tiny chuckle here, his declaration that when he's on stage, 'that's it, [I'm] complete' - but largely he revels in his fragmented condition. This, along with Alan Yentob's Cracked Actor, which aired on the BBC on January 26, 1975, would be the definitive portrayal of Bowie at his most alien form. But, in the sense that he is pushing the boundaries of his mental state, he is also recognizably David Bowie, just as the coked-out David seen by Keith Christmas was only another incarnation of the guy he knew in 1969. David had also phoned John Lennon and May Pang in his first few days back in New York; he was worried about meeting the ex-Beatle again, and at one point summoned Tony Visconti to the Sherry Netherlands hotel to help smooth the talk. Despite the fact that their encounter in LA had ended in failure, David and John had a lot in common. Bowie would regularly mention John; John was intrigued in David, pleasant, but always a little perplexed. 'David was still scared, but John was glad to hang out,' May Pang adds. The atmosphere remained uneasy, made even more so when Paul and Linda McCartney, who had just met John and May, arrived in mid-January.

Kramer noticed that in the studio, which they both enjoyed, John's empathy for David was palpable. 'Whatever stimulants he was using didn't hinder his ability to be creative,' says Kramer, who was present when Carlos Alomar began playing the riff, borrowed from a Rascals song, 'Jungle Walk,' that he'd added to the band's live version of 'Foot Stompin." 'David said, "I'll have that," or words to that effect, and he took Carlos' riff and turned it into a song.'

David had misheard shame' for 'fame,' a subject he'd been discussing with John earlier, as well as the title of yet another catastrophic MainMan effort, a Tony Ingrassia play that had just been released a few weeks previously. The misspelled word would be his biggest hit to date. Although several crucial recollections differ on whether Carlos started the vamp first and John joined in, Kramer, who witnessed David arrange the parts into a song after John had left the studio, says Bowie "was very much in charge, he knew exactly what he wanted." Part of Lennon's own guitar vamp remains in the three acoustic chords that introduce the song and punctuate the main theme before the last verse - F minor, C minor, and B flat. Carlos' riff, which was successful on "Foot Stompin," was the killer part on "Fame," but it's Bowie who makes it work - he plays the crunchy ascending guitar riff at the end of each line.

'Fame' is compulsive, boring, and claustrophobic, thanks to its reliance on a single chord. David had experimented with piano chords on Hunky Dory; now he was experimenting with sound itself, utilizing the studio as a huge cut-and-paste machine. The emotional impact was just as strong, because the song was a near-literal depiction of his existence, jumping from his ubiquitous anxieties about money - 'everything you need you have to borrow' - to his loneliness - 'takes you there where things are hollow'.

'Fame,' which had already been teased in the press as Fascination in December, would be the album's making; it would also arguably break it, because David felt compelled to include his version of 'Across the Universe,' the song that had inspired Lennon's arrival in the studio. The cover version was a shambles, worsened by David's warbling vocal, the most extreme example of his impersonation of Bryan Ferry and Scott Walker's styles so far, and a glaring weakness that the album's opponents would seize upon. (Lennon, like everyone else, was perplexed: 'Why that song?' he inquired of May Pang.) When 'Fame' became David's first number one single in the United States the following September, John was as excited as David. 'He had that competitiveness with the other men [i.e. Paul McCartney] - and he thought it was terrific,' adds Pang, who left John's life in February when the ex-Beatle returned to Yoko and The Dakota. May later married Tony Visconti, whom she met that winter at the Sherry.

The anticipation for the recording was one of the few bright spots in an otherwise miserable winter. David spent much of his Christmas in a coke-fueled haze with Tony Zanetta at the Sherry Netherlands. David had lost his final hope in Tony Defries and MainMan on November 18, the day the group made its spectacular entry - and dismal farewell - on Broadway. Tony Ingrassia, the brain behind Pork, wrote Fame, a chaotic, confused comedy based on the life of Marilyn Monroe. The MainMan circus had been founded by Pork; Fame, which closed after one performance, was its demise, as Bowie hated the reported $250,000 lost on its development, money his successes had produced. Conversations with John Lennon at the Electric Lady cemented David's decision. John had just dumped Beatles manager Allen Klein, which was honored by one of his final great songs, 'Steel and Glass,' which mocked Klein's LA tan and his infamous BO ('you leave your stench like an alley cat'). If John had had enough of Klein, David had had enough of Defries.

David attempted to reach Defries, who was away on his favorite island hideaway of Mustique, but was unable. They finally met in January. According to those close to them, the encounter was unusually dysfunctional, with neither man getting to the point. David informed acquaintances that Defries had accepted his choice to leave MainMan; Defries believed he had allayed David's fears and convinced him to stay. Defries would tell his pals how 'disappointed' he was with David in later months, as their split got increasingly acrimonious. He was let down by his ingratitude, his lack of grasp of commercial realities, and his drug addiction (for extra drama, he suspected David was also on heroin).

Over the next year, David would be plagued by disagreements with Defries, who would keep a portion of David's future releases for the balance of the MainMan contract period, right up to 1982, with the power to reject any album deemed uncommercial by Defries. Because of the harsh conditions, most observers automatically sided with David. Those who were present, however, confirm that Defries was not only a significant character in assisting Bowie's climb to prominence, but he was also an integral part of that period's unique magic.

David Jones had gone on a lengthy, arduous, and brutal quest to achieve recognition and success; many of his colleagues had exhibited similar ambition, but few had meticulously turned themselves from a mediocrity to an inspirational songwriter. He'd soon realize that the same things he'd worked so hard to create were now lost to him. David's pals believed that his final breakup with his one-time father figure would provide him "closure." Instead, it brought up a crisis.

Chapter 6: I Am Not a Weirdo

1977 had been a happy year, but it had been a peculiar type of happiness, one that many people would not recognize. David had avoided genuine labor as a youth, but now it was clearer than ever that as an adult, he valued the worthiness of studying, of good old Yorkshire graft. He'd tapped into his psychological reserves with intriguing effects during the Spiders era, but this second creative burst was possibly even more astonishing. There would never be another twelve months in Bowie's life as fruitful as those from the summer of 1976 to the summer of 1977, months in which he recorded four landmark albums: The Idiot, Low, Lust for Life, and "Heroes," all of which would have a huge impact on the musical landscape. David understood the significance of these records; he was filled with 'a peculiar kind of optimism' at the time, as Tony Visconti and others recall, in terms tinged with nostalgia. Even as he buried himself in work, David was aware that this particular time would not last.

He'd always moved quickly when he realized his musicians couldn't provide him anything else. But he was much harsher on himself, and even as he finished the final of his Berlin albums, he was destroying the lifestyle that gave rise to them.

David immediately launched an old-school advertising campaign following the publication of "Heroes." The single was released in three languages, evoking The Beatles' carefree early days, and David's promotion of the record took him to Rome, Amsterdam, Paris, and London, as well as, in September, to the Elstree TV studios outside of London, where venerable crooner Bing Crosby was recording a Christmas special for ITV. Swapping prepared jokes before duetting on 'Little Drummer Boy,' David seemed uncannily identical to the twenty-two-year-old who'd camped out on Malcolm Thomson's promotional film in 1969. While the language appeared to be phony, the jokey pleasantries and engaging politeness were genuine. Many of those who visited him during those weeks were taken aback to discover that, while serious, David was easygoing and pliant, rather than the aggressive, fairly megalomaniacal creature on exhibit early in 1976. Even when confronted with the most absurd questions, such as those made by radio interviewer John Tobler in January 1978, he maintained his composure. Tobler noted that, with the loss of Bing Crosby in November and Marc Bolan's sad accident in September, David's most recent colleagues had both perished shortly after working with him. 'Do you notice anything sinister about that?' Tobler was curious. 'No, I don't,' David responded with admirable patience before stating that Devo was the next act on his list - for production, not termination. His support for the band helped them land a Warner Brothers deal, albeit timing constraints meant that their debut album would be produced by Brian Eno.

David had a relaxing Christmas at Hauptstrasse in between rounds of interviews. According to the Berlin friends who attended, including Edu Meyer, Coco roasted goose for a cozy, joyful get-together. But it was their final Christmas break in Berlin, and it resulted in a public spat with Angie, effectively announcing the end of their marriage. On January 8, 1978, Angie complained to Tony Robinson of the Sunday Mirror that her husband had 'without my knowledge taken our son' from the Swiss house over Christmas. She'd actually left Zowie with Marion Skene as she went to see friends in New York. 'I want David to suffer,' she said to Robinson. 'Perhaps the only way he'll suffer is if I kill myself,' he says. Soon after the initial interview, she attempted suicide by taking sleeping pills and then smashing all of the glassware in the house before falling down the stairs, injuring her nose. According to Robinson, Angie supposedly caused so much uproar at the Samaritan's hospital that the woman in the adjacent bed, admitted following a cardiac arrest, relapsed.

Angie's official departure had minimal impact on David's romantic life. He'd relied on Coco for many of his requirements since his divorce from Ava Cherry in the summer of 1975, including companionship, jokes, protection, and domestic necessities, albeit she'd moved into her own modest flat in the Hinterhof, like Iggy. Both he and Iggy had the practice of leaving for a few days every now and then in Berlin, 'going where the drugs and girls were,' according to a buddy. 'David had his little muchachas, and Jim presumably had his as well. Coco would end up searching for them all around Berlin, worried that something had happened to them.'

In later years, Bowie would rarely mention his marriage to Angie; one of his most notable assessments was that it was "like living with a blowtorch." While his public comments were limited, his feelings about Angie eventually verged on mutual animosity; he would rarely address her by name, and simply referred to her as 'my ex-wife'. Her role in David's climb to popularity, like Tony Defries', would never be discussed again, as she was whitewashed out of his personal history. As a result, the grueling intensity of life with Angie had a predictable effect on his subsequent liaisons, which he would try to keep casual. There would be the odd preoccupation every now and then. He'd fallen in love with a boutique owner named Bessie while on tour with Iggy in Vancouver - 'beautiful, African, just as striking as [David's second wife] Iman,' according to Annie Apple, an old friend of Iggy's - and urged her to come back to Berlin with him. However, after accompanying him to Seattle, she was disturbed by the manic intensity that surrounded David; even while eating at a Shakey's Pizza Parlour in the suburbs, Bessie witnessed how followers would take his cigarette butts. Two days of this was exciting, but the prospect of more seemed terrifying. Soon after, David began dating another attractive black woman, an ex-girlfriend of Shep Gordon who remained with him in Vevey for a few days before being sent back home. David briefly dated Bianca Jagger, who was still married to Mick at the time, near the end of the year, with the kind of overdone secrecy that insured the word traveled far and wide. They made an appealing couple, but David's romance with her was short-lived due to the upcoming tour.

Instead, during his final months in Hauptstrasse, away from his tour entourage, David reveled in dressing anonymously, spending time with Zowie, still wandering down to the Kreuzberg clubs, smoking three packs of Gitanes a day, but also cycling on his Raleigh to 'pretty normal places, talking about life and the books he was reading,' according to Tangerine Dream drummer Klaus Krüger - whom David called up that spring, asking if he'd like

David began work on the film that would be his farewell to Berlin at the end of January 1978. David Hemmings created Just a Gigolo, his second film as a director after Blow Up. David was initially enthralled by the project, which represented many of his Berlin obsessions and was shot in and around his favorite spots, including Café Wien. Hemmings had pulled off a spectacular coup, which drew David into the project, by securing Marlene Dietrich for her first film in eighteen years. David had spent hours in Berlin talking to antique-store owners who'd met the secretive star back in the day; the idea of meeting her was a key element of the film's appeal.

Hemmings was upbeat and easygoing - his slogan was 'not too shabby, not too shabby' - and David told friends that he related more to the old-fashioned, hard-drinking luvvie than the more scholarly Nic Roeg. But it wasn't long before the shoot went wrong. Hemmings went missing during a celebratory supper with Bowie, other crew members, Iggy and Esther Friedmann. 'Something strange happened,' Friedmann says. '[Hemmings] went somewhere and never returned; people were looking everywhere. And David was never able to meet Marlene. He was actually acting with a chair instead of with her.'

Hemmings later indicated that Dietrich's brief cameo in the film would be shot in Paris; her side of the interaction with David was shot in a set resembling the Café Wien, and was intercut with his lines, which were delivered back in Berlin. The scene, like the film, was disjointed and irredeemably stilted; nonetheless, from a modern viewpoint, the film is a tragic last glimpse of the great German star, while David manages to appear attractive while carrying a pig.

Just a Gigolo's demise typified David's film career, which was more successful than that of rock-star rivals like Jagger and Sting but never came close to justifying his new job title, which he announced that year was 'generalist' - a term clearly influenced by, but lacking the charm of, Eno's 'non-musician' tag. The prospect of David's biggest tour to date provided a welcome distraction as Hemmings' problems mounted, with finance problems and negative reactions to his first edits all publicized in the movie press.

The Isolar II tour would put the flaky, tense zigzagging improvisation of the Ziggy era to shame, spanning four continents and featuring 78 dates, many of which took place in massive stadiums. The event was a grandiose, futuristic epic that featured the primarily electronic soundscapes of Low and "Heroes," but it also relied heavily on David's musical heritage. Natasha Korniloff was a Lindsay Kemp troupe acquaintance, and guitarist Adrian Belew was snatched from Frank Zappa's band. Simon House, David's guitarist from Turquoise, had hung out with David and Hermione in 1968 and played in High Tide with David. Sean Mayes met David through the band Fumble, who had rehearsed with him at Underhill and accompanied David on his Aladdin Sane tour in March 1973. Roger Powell, the keyboardist from Todd Rundgren's Utopia, joined the four Bowie veterans Alomar, Dennis Davis, and George Murray.

Carlos had spent six days at the Showco soundstage in Dallas running the band through a set based on Low and "Heroes" - brandishing a baton, like a classical conductor, for 'Warszawa' - before David arrived on March 19th after a brief vacation in Kenya and suggested they work up a sequence of Ziggy songs. The seven-piece band was solid but not overly polished, with Mayes' thumping piano lending a vital roughness to a string of well-received gigs.

The shows settled into a regular schedule over the course of three months. Every night, there'd be a frenzied dash to find a good restaurant or a club that was still open - Sean Mayes frequently served as a guide, hunting out homosexual places where David and the others might arrive later. Whereas the cavalcade had centered on Iggy and David during Station to Station, Carlos now behaved as the head of family, with David calm and amusing but distant. Meanwhile, business conflicts began to bubble around the modest crew's edges, between Coco and Pat Gibbons, or Pat and road manager Eric Barrett - a seasoned veteran best known for his work with Jimi Hendrix. The Mountains of Blow,' as Simon House recalls, did not help ease tensions. David rarely performed, but on one notable occasion in Paris on May 24, he stayed up for a twenty-hour coke bender after the first show; no one in the band noticed him until shortly before the second night's performance. Simon House was conversing in a dressing room doorway when he felt what felt like a psychic vibration behind him. Turning around, he saw the singer, pallid and clammy, his entire demeanor transformed - but the performance that night was spectacular.

The diverse English and American band members actually came together on stage, for an hour and a half of ecstasy, interspersed by musical communiqués or laughs. Dennis Davis was the main culprit, both on and off stage; he'd frequently try to leave the entire band helpless on stage, for example, by playing a tremendously lengthy drum fill, rolling over every drum in his kit in turn in a kind of manic protracted rhythmic monologue that would crease them all up. (Away from the stage, he was much the same, taking the mic anytime they were on the bus and offering a bizarre, surreal, pseudo-tour-guide commentary.) David loved it; he seemed to enjoy the energy of his band, who would periodically stare at him, transfixed by the spectacle. Even though David kept his distance from his bandmates - Sean Mayes referred to him as 'his Lordship' - there's a kind of affectionate attachment in their tales of sharing the stage with him: 'He has some power,' House says. 'An aura that allows you to communicate with thousands or millions of people. Freddie Mercury has it as well. Maybe it's just because they wrote such massive songs. But the music was always the highlight of this tour.'

Adrian Belew told House that he felt Bowie was "somewhat troubled." I'm not sure if he was still doing drugs or if he was just fatigued. I recall him as being lovely to be around in general, but I had the impression he was riding through it, not completely joyful.'

Simon House's recollections of the tour are far darker, for reasons unrelated to David. Sue, the violinist's partner, was suffering from Huntington's illness. Her dilemma was made all the more tragic because she refused to admit the condition that eventually landed her in the hospital and insisted on continuing with the trip. The condition expresses itself in various ways; in her case, she would be aggressive or inebriated, generating such a commotion in Tokyo that the hotel contacted the cops. David was understandably outraged if he spotted Sue on stage. House felt like an outcast as a result of it. Worse, because Bowie avoided directly addressing the subject, House was unable to explain Sue's condition. Carlos Alomar, as with most concerns, presented an almost spiritual, soothing attitude to such situations. 'Carlos is a psychologist, a spiritualist, and one of the most charming persons I've ever met,' House says. 'We got along pretty well; I wouldn't have enjoyed the tour without him. He was the one who would divert attention away from the difficulties.'

On the Station to Station tour, it was clear that David was the leader of a family; this time, it appeared that he was the head of a business empire. Coco and Pat Gibbons built the foundation of Isolar, David's management company, which evolved over the next five years but always had David at its pinnacle. David's ability to properly control himself distinguished him as a trailblazer in those early days, but that would change. The news that he would release a live album, mostly recorded in Philadelphia, while the tour was still rolling across Japan signaled the beginnings of his realization that he was a businessman as well as an artist. The double LP was meant to thwart bootleggers while also counting toward David's RCA requirement. The album's financial motivations were undeniably obvious - Jon Savage of Sounds summed it up best when he described Stage as a "combined summing-up, money-making, and time-gaining device" - but the audacity of the live show was evident as well, even in the album's first version, which was released with its tracks sliced and diced into chronological order.

By the time Stage was released on September 8, 1978, David had taken a brief break from his tour to work on the third album of a trilogy he'd announced in January. Trilogies, especially when rebranded as "triptychs," as David dubbed this set, risk outstaying their welcome, and Lodger lacked the spirit of risk and excitement that had suffused Low and "Heroes." Some of this was due to the venue: Mountain Studio in Montreux was carpeted, cozy, and boring in comparison to Hansa's edgy, uncomfortable air. Lodger, according to session regulars like Carlos Alomar, was a more academic, less inspired affair than "Heroes."

Eno had employed some of his Oblique Strategy tactics on the instrumental half of the previous album, most notably 'Sense of Doubt,' on the prior album. They were used for band recordings on this project - working title Planned Accidents - most notably in an exercise where Brian would point randomly at a chord chart on a wall and ask the musicians to play them. 'And then I'm thinking,

'This isn't going to replace a group chord chart that I can design,' Alomar recalls, 'and this experiment is stupid.'

'It sounded dreadful,' House says. 'Carlos had a difficulty, just because he's incredibly gifted and professional [and] he can't bring himself to play rubbish.'
'Come on fellas, play along!' David encouraged the hesitant guitarist, but the experiment was eventually abandoned. According to Tony Visconti, it was "not Brian's best idea." Carlos does admit that Eno's Oblique Strategy cards, which ordered random activities to avoid creative obstacles, performed as expected on other instances. 'One time, Brian asked me a question and I was blocked because I didn't understand what he was asking,' Alomar adds. 'Then one of the cards said, "Remember those silent moments," and another said, "Think like a gardener." Some strange, diverse references. It worked - or, let's say, you've come to accept it. I would have preferred to play something else, but it was enjoyable in retrospect.'

House was one of the few artists who had collaborated with Eno outside of Bowie - they'd recorded together on Robert Calvert's solo album - and admired Eno's inventiveness: 'He's always got an idea, is constantly on the case.' On this project, however, he believed that Eno's inspiration was fading, and that the primary purpose for his own usage of Oblique Strategies was to deal with his own artistic block, rather than the musicians'.

Eno's tendency seemed to be to experiment nearly indefinitely, and it was Bowie who showed decisiveness on this session, grabbing on one concept to keep things moving, impatiently overseeing the last few days when the true invention took place. The real beauty of the album came from the way random ideas were sprinkled like confetti over ordinary (and in some cases, repeated) chord structures: Adrian Belew's brilliantly warped guitar on 'Boys Keep Swinging,' for which the band all switched to unfamiliar instruments, a trick David and Carlos had first tried on Lust for Life; House's Byzantine violin, which influenced the Turkish vibe of 'Yassassin,' or the twisted One night Visconti took a bottle of Tequila and drew down an arrangement for three mandolins, which became 'Fantastic Voyage'.

'It was a great moment,' adds House, who co-starred with Belew and Visconti in the role.

The recording sessions were wonderful once the trials of the first few days were through, with the basic songs montaged from tape cuts. The tunes were shaped in the backdrop of a beautiful Indian summer, during which the musicians basked in the gorgeous view of Lake Geneva and spoke with Charlie Chaplin's grandson, Eugene Chaplin, who'd bring over trays of beer. 'It was the perfect fortnight,' House says. 'Although the music never quite gelled.' The violinist had high expectations, as he thought "Low and "Heroes" were ideal albums that couldn't be topped.

Adrian Belew arrived later in the recording process, after the backing tracks had been edited into shape. He was warmed up initially with a compliment. 'When I stepped in, David, Brian, and Tony were all smiling, as if they were sharing a secret. "What's going on?" I soon inquired. "When we did all the tracks with Robert Fripp for "Heroes," we did them as composite tracks," they explained. We grabbed something from each take and edited it all together to create something that could not be played. And you had no idea, and you did it all live!"'

The trio was praising him; knowing he'd done the impossible, he was expected to do the same in the session. Belew was taken upstairs to the recording studio, where Bowie, Eno, and Visconti kept an eye on him through a closed-circuit TV camera, with the guitarist's only contact with the outside world coming through his headphones.
Belew had just plugged in his Fender Stratocaster when he heard, 'The drummer will go 1, 2, 3, then you come in.'
'What key is it?' he inquired, his voice trembling.
'Don't be concerned about the key,' he was instructed. 'Just have fun!'

Lodger, which was completed in March 1979 at New York's Power Plant, was met with a respectable, slightly subdued reaction when it was released in May. Visconti attributed the lack of passion to a hurried mix. Much of the instrumentation did sound thin next to the joyful cacophony of "Heroes," as did the emotional substance, which was restless and eccentric where its two predecessors were deep. The album elicited admiration rather than visceral love or hatred, but its art-rock intellectualism fit in nicely with emerging bands like Talking Heads, who were produced by Brian Eno around the same time, or New Romantic bands like Spandau Ballet, whose Germanic name, sound, and peg-leg pants were all based on the 1978-model David Bowie.

The tour proceeded across Australia and Japan after a pause for the main Lodger sessions in September. For Belew, it was one of the most rewarding experiences of his career: 'We arrived in Japan and it was wonderful, like the stratosphere of super-fame.' Seven months of touring with David "really pushed me to become the guitarist I am today." In front of 20,000 people, he was the first to grant me permission to go explore. When you're in that situation, you nearly transcend yourself; you dig deep and discover things you didn't know were there. I was on a constant high.'

Lodger had a strong chart run, reaching number four in the UK and number twenty in the US, but despite the lull in his commercial momentum, David was well positioned, alongside Eno, as a patron of the late 1970s New Wave. Now in his thirties, he seemed to be moving faster from album to album than he had in his twenties - and the impressiveness of his achievement was underlined, if necessary, by the fate of his closest peers as New Wave patrons, namely Lou Reed and Iggy Pop.

Lou's music had spiraled into self-parody with Coney Island Baby and Rock and Roll Heart after the success of Transformer and its densely woven, emotionally grueling follower Berlin. Reed was out of ideas and money by the spring 1979 European tour, and he was drinking two pints of Scotch every three days, straight from the bottle.

Lou and David had only met on a few occasions since the MainMan days, but when Lou and his band learned that David would be appearing at Lou's Hammersmith Odeon performance in April 1979, they were ecstatic. The show was a shambles. When Lou noticed David sitting on an amplifier case at the side of the stage, he yelled at his players and moved the set around. But once he got to the last number, Lou was ecstatic, happy to meet his friend. Lou ran his hands affectionately over David's hair as the two hugged at the side of the stage before climbing into the tour bus and heading off in search of a meal.

When an iconic spat broke out at the Chelsea Rendezvous, the dishes were on the table. Lou was accompanied by his lover Sylvia, David by another woman, and Lou's guitarist Chuck Hammer, who overheard Lou asking David to produce his next record.
'Yes,' David said, 'provided you clean up your act.'

'Don't you ever say anything to me!' Lou struck David across the face, once on each cheek. Never, ever say that to me!' Lou's manager, Eric Kronfeld, dragged him away, and for a few moments, all was calm, until Lou slapped David again. This time, David's bodyguards separated them, and Lou and his friends were bundled out of the restaurant in seconds.

The scuffle, witnessed by a stunned Allan Jones of Melody Maker and Giovanni Dadamo of Sounds, would be covered in the respective music magazines, although neither journalist saw the following act of the drama. An hour or so later, Reed's band was back at the hotel, and guitarist Chuck Hammer was on the phone, telling a buddy about the night's events. He heard footsteps outside the passage, the sound of fists pounding on a nearby door, and then yells of 'Come on Lou - I know you're in there!'

For the first time since getting smacked in the eye by George Underwood, the man who had declared in 'Kooks' that he was 'not much cop at punching' was seeking to pick a fight. But, if he was in his room (no one knew), the dark prince of New York decadence stayed cowering under his blanket, and after a few more minutes of stomping up and down the corridor, David departed the building.

David was still 'devastated' a month later when he told Iggy and girlfriend Esther Friedmann about the fight, according to Friedmann. The episode demonstrated the dangers of assisting individuals you admire. Relationships with Iggy were also tense. The ex-Stooge had released one very successful album, New Values, on his own, but he'd been getting progressively despondent since then. David and Coco had tried to assist by taking him and Esther on vacation with them, including a trip to Kenya, 'but sometimes when people are wonderful to you, it's worse,' recalls Friedmann.

Iggy was in a bad position by September 1979, marooned in a domestic studio in Wales, lost in a cloud of heroin and liquor, and seemingly unable to complete the follow-up to New Values on his new label, Arista. David drove out with Coco to help, entertaining Iggy and the musicians with a long monologue about Johnny Binden, the thug, hanger-on, and owner of a legendarily large cock that he'd shown to David's former MainMain stablemate Dana Gillespie and Princess Margaret, among others, on Mustique. The story was then transformed into a song called "Play it Safe." Bowie was intimidatingly impressive - 'like a creative playmaster,' according to keyboard player Barry Andrews - but his presence seemed to underscore Iggy's struggle to navigate the business maze. Both men had comparable problems - egotism, jealousy, and a predisposition for musical postnatal depression once a project was over - but David's competitive mentality always spurred him to bounce back with a characteristic verve.

That competitiveness would add a satisfying edge to David's next project, for as Lou Reed's next album, Growing Up in Public, hit an artistic snag - leaving most of the music to collaborator Michael Fonfara and writing the lyrics drunk, by the studio pool - David was schmoozing Lou's guitarist, Chuck Hammer. 'Lou had really been an asshole [in London], and I was extremely pleased with David,' adds Hammer. He was the epitome of a gentleman. But later on, I wondered whether David was attempting to get back at Lou, to break up his band a little bit.'

Hammer would go on to contribute significantly to what many Bowie fans see as their hero's final truly great album. Scary Monsters still shines today, so there's plenty of basis for that viewpoint. Its strong, churning grooves feel startlingly contemporary - it's the clear root of Blur's angular rock attack from Park Life onwards - but despite the complexity of its arrangements, there are numerous moments of unadorned simplicity.

Scary Monsters was primarily recorded at New York's Power Station, widely considered as the best-sounding American studio of its time, signaling a departure from his European recordings. But, for the first time since Ziggy's reference to 1950s rock 'n' roll, the record also glanced back, at both Bowie's own career and the 'New Wave kids' who were emerging behind him.

According to popular belief, Bowie was determined to make a hit record. That was certainly the impression Chuck Hammer had, as he came to find a considerably more concentrated, almost conventional work ethic than in the previous Eno collaboration. David was still the confident, punctual young buck recalled by his buddies like The Manish Boys, despite being a renowned artist. David wore a full-length leather coat and Japanese sandals during the session, and he carried a clip-board on which he ticked off items on a musical 'to do' list. He was amusing, with that usual flirting jokiness, but with a formidable sense of intensity, just like in the Iggy sessions. Tony Visconti was almost frighteningly 'on it', recording and preparing ahead at the same time. 'They were an incredibly unified team,' Hammer says,'really wonderfully organized, no mayhem - but yet quite relaxed and creative.'

Hammer was brought in to work on a song called "People Are Turning to Gold." He'd been working on Guitarchitecture, a novel approach for building up synthesized layers, and had sent a cassette of his tests to Bowie. As he worked on the song, which had no lyrics at the time, he swiftly added characteristic 'choir' elements to the chorus before moving on to 'Teenage Wildlife' and the gospelly 'Up the Hill Backwards' (the latter part was removed, being replaced by Robert Fripp's excellent, frantic electric guitar). 'Chuck was very experimental for us; it was 50/50 whether he'd make the cut,' says Visconti, but Bowie drew out an inspiring performance from the young guitarist to offset the conventional electric guitar parts that Robert Fripp would record a few days later for the rest of the album. Bowie waited another two months before penning words for the song, which he eventually titled 'Ashes to Ashes': 'We like it a lot and knew it was going to be a big hit,' adds Visconti.

For all the arresting sonic effects laced throughout 'Ashes to Ashes,' it was the song's melodic inventiveness that underpinned its success: it represented a return to David's old-fashioned songwriting, with a swooping melody in the verse and one of his characteristic pre-verse digressions - 'the shriek of nothing is killing me' - as well as a conventional, but gorgeous middle eight, which even seemed

As a number one hit in the United Kingdom, 'Ashes to Ashes' seemed to indicate that Bowie would dominate the 1980s as thoroughly as he had the 1970s. He commandeered the Blitz club scene for the video, which was an integral aspect of the single's final popularity - a scene that, of course, used Bowie's style as a blueprint. In one of the first times he interacted with a new generation of artists he'd influenced, he was the epitome of charm, dropping in for an evening with the club's host Steve Strange, then inviting him to the next day's 6am trip to Southend for the celebrated video shoot, which reprised Lindsay Kemp's Pierrot style, again with a costume designed by Natasha Korniloff. Now thirty-three, he was easygoing and gregarious - and, as Steve Strange proudly states, 'when he snogged me, I got some tongue, too'. If David had intended to retaliate against Lou Reed, he must have thought that two-timing him with his guitarist and achieving a number one would have put him in his place.

Scary Monsters' final success was poignant for everyone involved. Even as a slew of bands attempted to replicate Scary Monsters' gritty electro-funk mashup, the majority of those responsible, including drummer Dennis Davis and bassist George Murray, were looking for new work. Tony Visconti, on the other hand, would not work with David again for another twenty-one years, except for a brief session in Berlin. 'It's one of my favorite Bowie albums ever,' says the producer. 'I thought it would end on a high note.'

For David, the album represented a welcome change of scenery; he had never officially left Berlin, but he was energized by his return to New York, where he could hang out with a younger generation of arty New Wavers, and also rekindled his friendship with John and Yoko, under happier, more relaxed circumstances for both of them. The success of 'Fame,' which had put the ex-Beatle back on the charts, had only strengthened John's admiration for David. David still saw John as his closest role model, alongside Mick Jagger, but his affection for John was not tinged with jealousy, as it was with Mick. David recognized that Lennon had brought out a finer side of him. Fortunately, John had resumed his writing. David appreciated the distinctive lifestyle he'd created for himself and Yoko, centered on their magnificent, white-carpeted, simply furnished apartment in The Dakota, close to Central Park, where John and Yoko could stroll uninhibitedly.

As David finished what would become an everlasting masterpiece, he began work on another, more fleeting achievement. When he received a call from Jack Hofsiss, director of The Elephant Man, a production based on the life of Joseph Merrick that David had seen in New York in February, the Scary Monsters sessions were in full swing. Hofsiss was looking for a replacement for Philip Anglim, who was leaving the title role. The play had taken Bowie by surprise, and with only twenty-four hours to decide, he agreed to play the part.

Before the group gathered in San Francisco for a fortnight of hard work, David spent time rehearsing one-on-one with Hofsiss. His casting was classic celebrity casting, as it is still done today, so when David arrived at the Geary Theater, there was a chance that Bowie's fellow actors would have disliked being upstaged by an upstart rock 'n' roller. Especially Ken Ruta, a stalwart of the American Conservatory Theatre and a fan of Gielgud and Tennessee Williams, who played Merrick's friend and benefactor, Doctor Frederick Treves, night after night. Ruta, on the other hand, is clear about his leading man. 'He was amazing. 'You're dead on.'

As one listens to The Elephant Man cast's recollections, echoes of David's time on the road with the Lindsay Kemp company a dozen years previously emerge. Kemp recalls that 'he was not starry at all, by God no.' Ruta is also emphatic: 'He was absolutely not a show-off,' she says, echoing co-star Jeanette Landis. 'He was an extremely pure actor. In fact, he was more professional than the actor he was replacing.'

For a few months, the location reminded Bowie of his late teens, when he was part of Kemp's small crew. Bowie was well aware that the England that feted and mocked Merrick still existed, thanks to his upbringing among the magnificent Victorian edifices of Brixton or The Lower Third's performances alongside the bearded lady side-shows of Margate. David had gone to the London Hospital before rehearsals to study Merrick's bones and the sad cardboard church he'd built, which - in bigger form - is a highlight of the play, a symbol of Merrick's quest for beauty and serenity. Most of the actors in the play, including David, felt sympathy for Merrick, which was heightened by the presence of people who had suffered from his condition in the audience. What they didn't expect was to find such surprising connections between Merrick, the circus freak, and their leading man's lives.

Parts of David's routine were standard. On Sundays, he'd pick up the New York Times and go through the book reviews. Later in the week, he'd spread out each of the novels that had garnered wonderful reviews on a table in front of him; he'd soon have read them all. At the end of each week, he'd give a small gesture of affection to his fellow performers. 'It depends on your diversion preferences,' adds Ruta. 'Normally, I get a nice bottle of red wine.' He'd wander down to a tiny milk bar he'd discovered when the show opened in Denver, just to unwind or dance with some younger company.

He also appeared to readily learn the routine on stage. There were numerous little hiccups at first, none of which disrupted the flow. 'He hadn't acted on a stage, so the acting method wasn't fully within his control,' explains Ruta, 'but, thank God, he had such an imagination, so the integrity was there. There was a fundamental honesty. And the biggest gift of any great actor, in my opinion, is the ability to listen. That doesn't happen every time.' It's a remarkable observation, because what else could Bowie have been doing when recording Low or "Heroes" but listening - picking out sounds and making sense of them?

'He seemed to have captured that - better than all the other ones who wanted to be glamorous,' his co-stars said of Bowie's physical change into Merrick. He wasn't going for the glitz. 'He was doing Merrick,'

Jeanette Landis says. Ken Ruta then saw John Hurt play Merrick in The Elephant Man, swamped under a prosthesis, and found the experience significantly less engaging than watching David.

The play had already been a hit before David's presence; US President Jimmy Carter was a fan of the book, and he and his wife had come to meet the initial cast. However, when David came over for Anglim, the upstart replacement improved the game. 'Whatever that thing was - it wasn't anything practiced or created - it was there,' Ruta explains. Variety's account of the opening night performance in Denver confirms Ruta's memories of the event. 'Bowie commands the stage with authority,' said one reviewer. 'He has a rapid and sensitive voice.'

When David branded himself as 'the actor' on the sleeve of Hunky Dory, it felt like a conceited remark. He has now attained the title. In the restless world of the theater, where actors form friendships and then move on to the next play, he was a much more sympathetic figure to his coworkers, who, like musicians, rarely expect their working ties to continue. According to the Denver and Chicago cast members, Bowie was "a honey." He was good, kind, and brilliant, and he worked for his money.' Jeanette Landis, his starring lady, was equally taken with him. 'His brilliance was greater than his ego, which is unusual.'

There was, however, a schism between David and the other actors. It was a chasm that was barely discernible during their week in Denver, where they broke the theater's box office record. However, from the moment the troupe arrived in Chicago on August 5, 1980, the conditions in which Bowie was compelled to reside horrified his comrades. He, like Merrick, led the life of a freak. 'I had a good time in Denver, which was more or less the Hinterlands. 'It was terrifying in Chicago,' adds Ruta. 'Unrelenting mobs of people.' Jeanette Landis recalls, 'It was out of control.'

David was obliged to travel to the Blackstone Theatre in a garbage truck, sneaking in and out through a basement window, within days. With admirers following him around the city's major hotels, he chose to stay in a flat above a neighboring department store. Only a few cast members were aware of its location. Most of his clothes were taken at one point during the run: 'He basically had a tacky T-shirt, a pair of pants, and a cardboard suitcase,' adds Ruta. 'It was the most dreadful, horrible life I'd ever known.'

The supporters' constant attention, viewed up close, was unnerving because it was persistent. It would never let up during the Chicago run. Ruta and Landis collaborated extensively with security officers recruited to protect the cast for the first time in their careers. According to Ruta, Coco, who was viewed as intrusive by many of David's musicians, was a "proteress" in this setting. 'Wonderful. She looked after him.'

After a few days, the cast would scan the first few seats as they stepped onto stage, wondering who would be there. One night, a fan placed an object on the stage, and Bowie ordered Ruta, 'Leave it, don't touch it,' while they grabbed a few words in the wings. Ruta obeyed him, caught up in the frantic, menacing environment.

Ruta saw a distinct group of fans in the front row at the finish of the Chicago run. 'About six girls, all strange looking, this was before punk turned insane, all with colored hair, all carrying purses in their laps,' she says. They were there all week, for both the Saturday matinée and the evening performance. Then, as the actors took the curtain call at the end of the performance, all six girls rose, purses in hand, and made their way to the stage. 'It was quick, they were all tackled from the sides by I don't know how many plainclothes men. And they had something metallic in their purses - they were going to do something nasty. That night was just coo-coo.' Security escorted the females out of the premises, and Ruta never learned what they were up to, but he believes they were out to scare David - or worse.

After a two-week break for rehearsals and the installation of a higher-profile supporting cast, the show transferred to New York on September 23, 1980, and the curtain opened to a star-studded audience that included Christopher Isherwood, Andy Warhol, David Hockney, Aaron Copland, and David's Montreux neighbor - and supposed lover - Oona Chaplin. The New York reviews were mainly positive or appreciative, and with Scary Monsters at number one in the UK chart and number twelve in the US, Bowie appeared to have attained the sort of cross-cultural symbol to which, despite too many protests, he clearly aspired. Friends like John, Yoko, Iggy, Esther, and May Pang pressed at the dressing room door after the initial performances, gushing about his stage debut. Throughout the month, journalists from hefty tomes like the New York Times and London periodicals like The Times and Sunday Times waited up for their fifteen-minute slot, which was overseen by Barbara and Tim Dewitt. In multiple interviews, he praised New York's invisibility; like his friend John, he liked how you could go around the city unnoticed. 'The most you get is, "Hi Dave, how's it going?" he told Patricia Barnes of The Times.

May Pang called David Bowie's Chelsea residence on December 8, exactly two weeks after The Times interview, to inform him that John Lennon had been shot dead by Mark Chapman. Coco picked up the phone. 'David is out on a date,' she explained to May. 'Come down here right now. You shouldn't be by yourself.'

David arrived about the same time as May at the apartment. 'WHAT THE HELL, WHAT THE FUCK IS GOING ON WITH THIS WORLD!' she recalls him yelling. over and over, enraged, devastated, and numb. At times, all of them had flashbacks or fleeting convictions that this was all a prank and hadn't actually happened; they'd repeatedly urge each other, 'We have to be calm, we can't allow our emotions take over.' David sat in front of the TV, transfixed by news footage of distressed fans lingering about The Dakota skyscraper and Central Park after crying himself to numb acceptance. When May Pang left the flat about daybreak, he was still awake. As she walked home, New York was eerily silent.

David appeared in The Elephant Man for the majority of the final three weeks, missing only a few nights. He'd describe it as 'terrible, just dreadful' two years later. 'A whole element of my existence seemed to be taken away; a complete reason for being a singer and songwriter seemed to be ripped away from me. It was almost as though it was a warning.' There were unsubstantiated rumors that Mark Chapman had seen a performance of The Elephant Man or had made a list of targets that included David Bowie and Keith Richards.

Whatever the truth was, the death of the one man with whom he most identified in New York left David with only one option: flee.

Chapter 7: Fuck off, it's my life.

By the end of 1987, David had moved on from his grief over Glass Spider's death. He was preoccupied with a much more serious matter: a lawsuit filed by a lady called Wanda Lee Nichols, who accused Bowie of sexually abusing her in a Dallas hotel room on October 9, 1987.

In terms of David's immediate social group, if he had deep-seated concerns about his profession, he kept them to himself, but he didn't keep his concerns about the Nichols case to himself. 'It was a big deal,' one friend says. 'He's not invincible; it rattled the Hell out of him.' It wasn't so much the precise accusation - which was strange in retrospect, alleging he'd bitten the woman and then mentioning he had Aids - as it was what it symbolized. He admitted to sleeping with Nichols but said the rest of her tale was made up. From now on, while he was enjoying the typical reward of his employment in a hotel room, he was constantly worried about another accusation and a lengthy lawsuit.

Despite the fact that a grand jury rejected to indict him a month later, the accusation hung over David for over three years until being dropped. In the early weeks after Nichols' charges became public, David found a much-needed friend in the person of Sara Terry, Glass Spider's press representative. Terry, a Christian Science Monitor journalist, had joined the tour for a respite after concluding a grueling project on child prostitutes and soldiers. She was a straightforward, respected adviser, described by pal Eric Schermerhorn as 'cool, forceful, subtle, and intellectual - an alpha female just like Coco'.

Sara's husband, Reeves Gabrels, joined the tour as well; not as rigorous as his wife, he was very quiet, nice, hilarious, bashful, brilliant, one of those Americans with no mental limitations,' according to musician friend Kevin Armstrong. Reeves, who studied guitar at the famed Berklee College of Music, had previously spent three years at art school. He'd never told David about his musical ambitions since he assumed he was a painter, but in the closing days of the tour, Sara smuggled David a cassette recording of Gabrels' band, The Dark. Sara returned to the Christian Science Monitor after the tour and relocated to London with Reeves. David checked out the tape in January 1988 and soon began recommending Gabrels for sessions. Then, in June, it became clear that he also required the services of a guitarist. David Bowie was suddenly in a hurry again. 'It happened incredibly fast,' Gabrels says. 'David called me, I flew to Switzerland, and we had this song to finish in a weekend,' she says.

The project was a collaboration with the dance troupe La La La Human Steps; Reeves created an arrangement for 'Look Back in Anger,' with an extended, dark, clipped instrumental passage: 'Because we'd only really talked about art before, when we did start working together, all our reference points for sound were painterly or architectural. David kept saying things like, "We should do something where the guitars are like flying buttresses and cathedrals."

The first obvious sign that Pepsi-sponsored, pre-planned Bowie had given way to art-house, improvisational Bowie came in an inconspicuous but renowned performance at London's Dominion Theatre in July 1988. The nine-minute performance with the Quebec dance group was part of a benefit for the London ICA arts center; Bowie learned his dance moves in two days, primarily as a counterbalance to the lithe, muscular Louise Lecavalier. As Lecavalier leaped over him or cradled him on her knees like a doll, while Gabrels, Armstrong, and Erdal Kizilcay sang their twisted, gothic, drawn-out version of the old Lodger song, there was a genuine sense of danger and sexuality that had long been missing from his music. The concert was a convincing reminder of David's ability to wrest meaning from seemingly random strands.

Gabrels returned to Lausanne for a weekend visit two weeks later. He decided to stay for a month. 'Every day, we'd travel down to Montreux's Mountain Studios and simply work on stuff. Then return home for dinner. Then watch Fawlty Towers before going to bed.'

The pair's conversation in July 1988 would establish the framework for David Bowie's next decade. The singer was candid, bright enough to recognize his problem, and honest enough to admit it. He informed Gabrels that, following his massive agreement with EMI, he felt obligated to deliver hits - 'and it was kind of killing him,' Gabrels adds. They talked and spoke, looking for the influences that drew David to music in the first place. In that desire to rediscover that old sensation of exhilaration, the idea for the Tin Machine band project arose. 'If there was a plan, David just wanted to make the music he wanted to make,' explains Gabrels. 'One amazing thing was that we were all listening to the same things: Led Zeppelin bootlegs, Cream bootlegs, Hendrix bootlegs, Miles Davis' Bitches Brew, Coltrane, the Pixies, Sonic Youth, Glen Branca, Stravinsky, John Lee Hooker, Buddy Guy, Junior Wells, and Muddy Waters. Put everything in a blender, and you've got a Tin Machine.'

The two began talking just a few days before a chance meeting that summer, when David was launching a video of the Glass Spider tour. Tony Sales, Iggy's ex-bassist, stepped up to David and surprised him. And then we were in Switzerland doing Tin Machine a few weeks later.'

The bassist's description of David as merely 'a friend' contrasts with the aloof, selfish figure described by predecessors such as Trevor Bolder, although his view is not unusual. The classic version of Tin Machine's formation is a Bowie-centered one in which he uses them to unleash a controlled explosion, erasing the memory of his late-eighties arrogance. Yet, according to Sales, the desire to spend time with his friends and assist them was a significant motivator. Tony and his drummer brother, Hunt, arrived in Montreux Casino and spent a week hanging out and playing with David, Reeves, and producer Tim Palmer before deciding they needed a second guitarist. Kevin Armstrong, who, like Tony Sales, was trying to repair his life after becoming a groupie-shaggin', drug-sniffing' rock-monster during his last tour with Iggy Pop, answered the call and did a double-take as he entered the massive room. The most crucial hint to the band's psychological make-up was in front of him, in the form of a line of amplifiers - for Reeves, Tony, Armstrong, and David - all facing a massive platform in the middle of the room. Hunt Sales' drum kit, with its massive twenty-four-inch bass drum, was perched above the podium, which could be reached via a ladder. Without any electronic aid, the feisty, hilarious, mad drummer could beat anyone into submission with this kit: 'He is the loudest drummer I have ever worked with,' Kevin Armstrong adds. 'Within the first couple of days, I practically went deaf. The power and volume were simply out of this world.' Producer Tim Palmer had meticulously arranged mics around the studio to catch this huge sound, and they penned and recorded 'Heaven's in Here' on Armstrong's first day.

When David recorded with the Sales brothers and Iggy in Berlin, the cultural leitmotif was expressionism, Fritz Lang, and Das Neue Sachlichkeit. Eleven years later, in Montreux, the subject was Soupy Sales: the foul-mouthed, sexist, undeniable comedy genius who, of course, inspired The Simpsons' Krusty the Clown, the kids' entertainer with a filthy mind. During the Mountain sessions, the Sales sons would call their father on an international line and route the call through the studio monitors, while David, Hunt, Tony, Kevin, and Reeves would collapse from laughter at monstrously amplified jokes like: What do 50,000 battered wives have in common?
They don't give a fuck!

Bowie deferred to Reeves more than anybody else; he lauded his experimentation, his stunt' guitar, and his dexterity, encouraging him to pursue more extreme effects and sounds. Despite his position as Bowie's lieutenant, Gabrels had little influence on his rhythm section. When the Sales brothers joined, David determined the band should be run like a democracy. Gabrels perceived it to be more of a shouting match.

The band's initial Montreux jam sessions easily transitioned into a recording endeavor, with 'Heaven's in Here' recorded on the first day, then became semi-formalised with a move to Compass Point - a recording studio in the Bahamas, where David remained in Robert Palmer's house near the beach. The jam sessions continued indefinitely; they were not aimless or desperate, but just jams, with dozens of tracks reportedly recorded. Sean Lennon dropped by over the school holidays with Joey, who was about to leave Gordonstoun. Despite his academic issues, Joey was a quiet, unspoiled youngster who loved The Smiths - David claimed to be a fan, but Joey was skeptical. It was hilarious for the band to see a man they thought was the coolest dad in the world attempting to impress his son. Sean, too, was earnest, thoughtful, and the polar opposite of a showbiz brat; the band recorded their own rendition of John's 'Working Class Hero' in his honor.

The small community gathered at the beach was augmented by David's new girlfriend, Melissa Hurley, a Glass Spider tour dancer. The Sales brothers, true rock 'n' rollers, hardly spoke to Melissa. Kevin Armstrong liked her because she was a genuinely pleasant, sweet person.' She was just twenty-two years old and had a voluptuous, almost Italian shape with a profusion of wavy dark brown hair. She was kind and not aggressive. She also had a typical 1980s fashion sense that clashed with David's polished elegance; she purchased him hats or brilliantly colored scarves that he would wear for a few days before losing. He, as a globe citizen and something of an art teacher manqué, loved showing her new places and recognizing her delight; together, they seemed carefree, almost childlike, and it was no surprise when Melissa's parents revealed the couple had been engaged in May 1989.

David's indulgence of his new girlfriend was endearing, especially at the more absurd instances, such as when Melissa convinced him to wear a thong, which he did a couple of times on the beach, oblivious to his bandmates' sniggers. Another amusing feature was the presence of hoary old British rockers Status Quo, who were working in the adjacent studio and were always willing to teach pool and table football. The unspoiled, carefree atmosphere was due in part to rumors that Coco, a frequent source of conflict between David and his band, had found love and was living with a lawyer in Los Angeles.

However, the environment was not a tropical paradise for one of the band members. A week or two into the sessions, David walked over to Kevin Armstrong's beach hut and told him that Tin Machine was intended as a four-piece, and that they'd like to retain Armstrong on as a background musician. The news was 'absolutely heartbreaking' for the musician. Nonetheless, David's man-management was better than in the past; he was honest and forthright about Armstrong's relegation, telling him they'd work together again after Tin Machine, which they did.

Tin Machine had its public debut at Compass Point, where they were conversing and hanging out when they felt it would be a good idea to play live. Later that night they strolled up to the band playing a small bar in Nassau and asked if they could borrow their gear; forty or fifty shocked American tourists goggled at the spectacle, mouthing at each other, 'Is that who I think it is?' as the band played a short performance featuring 'Heaven's in Here'. 'It was a shambles, but it was a wonderful buzz,' Armstrong adds, 'simply to see the reaction of the fans.' David loved the mood, the raw exhilaration of what they all called 'the guerrilla gig,' and they all agreed that was how the band would go forward: a tiny gang, one for all, all for one.

Of course, there could never be a really equal group. On the 14th of June, 1989, when the band finally began their club tour in New York, David Bowie handed each of them $1000 to buy a Prada outfit for the event. And when the Tin Machine album was released on May 22, 1989, it was inevitably perceived as another David Bowie record, rather than the premiere of a new band. The album received generally excellent reviews, with Q magazine's Paul du Noyer calling it "a more accessible sort of record than we're used to," while fans were overjoyed at the idea of seeing David Bowie perform on a club tour. They waited in line for two days for some of the European dates, which took place at modest venues such as Amsterdam's Paradiso and Kilburn's National Ballroom. David was energized by the enthusiasm of the crowd and the sheer freedom. But there was also friction; he was always wary of admirers. Kevin Armstrong had played with Iggy in similar-sized venues and saw he had a knack for soothing off any disturbed or high fans; he could merely touch their shoulder, like a Vulcan death-grip, and they'd go all limp. David had never worked under those conditions; by the time he began gathering real crowds in his Ziggy days, he had his own security team. When surrounded by fans, he'd be nice and pleasant; if they were too pushy, he'd simply blank them, but he was always wary, never nearly as relaxed amid the chaos as Iggy.

The shows themselves were 'crazed and great fun,' according to Armstong, and 'a blast,' according to Tony Sales. Most proper bands, however, gel as they do more shows. 'There was no gelling with Tin Machine,' explains Armstrong. Because it was a fight, it never really gelled musically. Hunt and Tony were the most consistent characters, followed by Reeves, who is a complete mess - but Reeves and Hunt did eventually build a relationship. But you never knew what was going to happen; it was always tense. Because Tony's short-term memory is bad, I was shouting the chords to him most evenings. You couldn't possibly play the same music twice. It wasn't at all comfy for me.'

According to Iggy, David's old rhythm section didn't produce the same results: 'I have to say, when they were with me, they swung more.' Indeed, there was a monotonous, dogmatic element to Tin Machine gigs, as evidenced by songs like their sluggish cover of "Working Class Hero." This worthiness, combined with Kevin Armstrong's lamentable rejection of 'traditional' tunes, meant that Tin Machine's initially warm welcome - which peaked at number three in the UK and number twenty-eight in the US - quickly faded. The emergence of lumpen singles like 'Under the God,' backed by a workmanlike cover of Dylan's 'Maggie's Farm,' accelerated the process. Democracy is not without flaws. 'Sometimes a benign dictatorship can be a wonderful thing,' says Gabrels.

But there was a certain energy about the band for David; he adored the Sales brothers' atmosphere and Hunt's special crazy. Gabrels thought the same thing at first: 'They were like Dean Martin and Jerry Lewis,' he adds. 'Quite a handful. Then, during Tin Machine, they were transformed into Cain and Abel. They added a lot of tension and amusement if you find stress entertaining.' Hunt had his manifesto tattooed on his back one night in New York: 'It's My Life' in large letters. But that wasn't the end of his manifesto; he'd meant to have the words 'so fuck off' written underneath, but told his bandmates that the hefty Gothic script was too painful after the first three sentences.

Tin Machine's unavoidable issue is that its democratic concept was a Utopia. Bowie was usually blamed for Gabrels' or the Sales brothers' artistic blunders, yet their ideas and innovations were also credited to him. Meanwhile, EMI had paid a large advance for the David BowieTM brand rather than Tin Machine, which would eventually cause financial difficulties. Meanwhile, the man at the center of these paradoxes was content to enjoy the experience for what it was. 'I don't believe David was frustrated at any point,' Armstrong says. 'Everyone was aware that he could simply whip this magic carpet away, but you can't avoid letting the Sales brothers do their thing while it was there, because they are really powerful people.'

David's easygoing attitude toward Tin Machine's internal disputes was logical, given that he could always rely on Brand Bowie. Even as the band was booking tiny club shows in the spring of 1989, Isolar and Bill Zysblat, now Bowie's business manager, were penciling in stadiums all over the world for a year later, while David was simultaneously planning for the re-release of his RCA records.
In 1989, most record labels had extracted maximum money from fans who were moving from vinyl to CD. The Beatles' and Stones' CD reissues were both a shambles; Bowie's re-mastering of his LP collection, on the other hand, was excellent. He chose CD specialists Rykodisc to master the records and distribute them in Europe, while EMI licensed them in the United States.

The new editions were a lesson in CD releases, with rarities and exquisite packaging, while a Sound + Vision box set served as a sort of alternative best hits, with outtakes or other versions. If there was any inconsistency in the fact that one of the world's most forward-thinking artists was among the first to re-market his own history, it was disregarded, given how much better he did it than his colleagues. The election of Bill Clinton as President of the United States in January 1993 marked the beginning of the baby boomers' ascendancy to power. This generation, including Bowie admirers, had more disposable income than any previous generation. Experts such as David and Bill Zysblat, who would soon lead the way in promoting stadium tours with his company RZO, maximizing their financial returns, were on hand to assist them in spending it.

Within the first few months of Tin Machine's existence, David discussed the idea of a greatest hits stadium tour with Reeves

Gabrels. However, the guitarist felt that 'it didn't feel like my place to do it'. Appearing on stage with David for a greatest hits tour would also make Tin Machine appear to be a side project, so Gabrels suggested a musician he knew and liked who also had a connection to Bowie's back catalog: Lodger guitarist Adrian Belew.

Sound + Vision was another ground-breaking tour, perfectly organized, brilliantly choreographed - by Édouard Lock of La La La Human Steps - and presented with cutting-edge video technology. A sparsely decorated stage was flanked by a massive screen showing video footage, much of it a large moving picture of David himself, with which the real singer would interact. The tour was marketed as the first and only time David would perform a 'Greatest Hits' set, and it occurred during a period when 10 of his reissued albums all charted in the United Kingdom. According to musical director Adrian Belew, what would effectively be Bowie's final grandstanding stadium tour was' sensational' for both the musicians and the audience. 'We'd walk out and start playing "ground control to Major Tom," and the emotional feeling would overwhelm you, then there'd be the video, the lights, and all these gigantic images floating around - it would absolutely give you the shivers.'

After eighteen years of traveling, David Bowie's live shows were anything but fantastic for the artist who had informed his management as a youngster that he despised "ballrooms and the kids." Several times during the Sound + Vision tour, which lasted from March 4 to September 29, 1990, David would ask his manager, "Why do David Bowie and Mick Jagger both feel compelled to keep going out touring?" Why are we doing this? It's ridiculous.' The subject was brought up multiple times, but there was no resolution, according to Belew.

When David called Belew, he used all of his charm, even recommending Adrian's own band, which included drummer Mick Hodges and keyboardist Rick Fox. For Belew, it was a "dream come true" to accompany his band and childhood pals on tour, and he felt "like a kid with a handful of candy."

The tour, on the other hand, was 'awful' for bassist Erdal Kizilcay. The contradicting accounts were due to a simple reason: whether you were in front of or behind the screen. Belew would be Bowie's principal foil in the stripped-down visuals, with the other three remaining unseen: 'It was awful for them when they found out,' Belew recalls. 'They get to play with David Bowie while no one can see them.'

A sponsorship arrangement planned for the opening dates in Canada demonstrated the seemingly insurmountable conundrum of David's desire for both cult status and mainstream money, according to Erdal Kizilcay. In 1987, David drew scorn for accepting the Pepsi money. The sponsorship of the first Canadian leg of the new tour by Labatt proved more detrimental. According to the agency who arranged it, the arrangement featured a pause in the set for the sponsor's message, which fatally undermined its momentum. 'It was horrific,' adds Erdal Kizilcay, 'many left the venue - and didn't come back. I'm not sure how much he got for it, but it blew up the concert's high point, the middle fifteen minutes. You'd return and have to start warming up the people all over again, and the answer was, 'No way.'

Belew doesn't recall the sponsorship slot being the main issue; rather, the design of a clear metal stage with amplifiers buried beneath, combined with the four-man lineup, meant that the music would always come in second place to the unique aesthetics. 'I was fairly unhappy with myself and what we were able to do musically throughout the tour. We were working with a small band, so how do you play "Young Americans" without a saxophone? Mike, Rick, and I had just returned from a club tour where the sound is warm and everyone can hear you... here it seemed metallic, with a thin guitar tone. I wish I could say I did a better job.'

Despite the technological difficulties, David and Adrian remained upbeat for the duration of the tour; for the backstage lads, despite getting to utilize Chrysler CEO Lee Iacocca's private plane for numerous dates and staying in fancy hotels, it was tedious. During the show, keyboardist Rick Fox was frequently limited to just pressing a button to play a sample or sequence; as a result, if he was hungry mid-set, he'd eat a sandwich or a burger. Erdal then observed

David make a gesture in the middle of 'The Jean Genie' and mistook it for a signal to come out from behind the curtain, which he did. 'Then David yelled at me, "Get off!" It seemed strange.'

According to Belew, while the band sat on the plane after the gig, David 'raged and yelled' at Erdal, and "a quiet came over everyone." We just sat in the plane. It was dreadful.'
It was a one-time occurrence, but it demonstrated how, for many musicians, 'you start with a lot of fire and enthusiasm, but gradually you wear down,' Belew explains. 'But that scene with Erdal was the only one, which is very good for a group of 45 people traveling around the world.'

David made a real effort to enjoy the tour - he was more enjoyable to be around than in 1978, and took Belew out for a memorable night in Paris, where he and Mick Jagger sought to out-camp each other on the dancefloor in that characteristic blend of friendliness and schoolboy rivalry. Throughout, he'd pump up Adrian and focus on stretching him as a musician, all while attempting to figure out how he could tour without being formulaic. He didn't complain, but it was clearly hard work for him, even if the band didn't believe his well publicized declaration that this would be the last time he'd play his hits live; rather, it appeared to be a good marketing gimmick. David had instituted a telephone poll, asking fans to nominate their favorite songs for inclusion in the set, and as the tour approached Europe, the NME launched a campaign to lobby for the inclusion of 'The Laughing Gnome'; he was unfazed by their cheekiness (though, sadly, they never played the song). Even as the tour rumbled through Europe before concluding in South America, he remained far less agitated than on the 1978 tour, joking and singing Beatles songs throughout.

Throughout the second half of the tour, it was clear David was having problems with Melissa; this added to his chemistry with Belew, with whom he'd talk about his problems - his honesty, the fact that he was still having girl problems at forty-three, was charming. The band loved Melissa -'she was a great person, but maybe not strong enough for David,' says Erdal, who'd also seen her sometimes in Switzerland - but she sat on the bus by herself for the subsequent European performances. She then vanished. David was courteous about the separation, saying he was concerned it would become a 'older guys, younger girl situation' and described her as such a fantastic, lovely, bright girl'. Melissa eventually married Patrick Cassidy, the brother of 1970s teen idol David.

Whatever the backstage squabbles, the end of the Sound + Vision tour was a life-changing experience for David, the significance of which he realized a few weeks later, on September 29, 1990, at Buenos Aires' River Plate Stadium. Teddy Antolin, a hairdressing acquaintance, had set up a blind date for David on October 4th. Later, David would say it was love at first sight, despite the fact that he had met his date three or four times before, in the theater and backstage at his May show in Los Angeles.

Iman Abdul Majid was an eighteen-year-old political science major at Nairobi University when wildlife photographer Peter Beard, a friend of writer Isak Dinesen, happened to spot her in May 1975; she eventually agreed to her first photoshoot in exchange for having her tuition fees paid, and caused a sensation when she signed with the prestigious Wilhelmina Models agency upon her arrival in New York. Iman collaborated with Thierry Mugler and was a muse for Yves Saint-Laurent. She rose to prominence in the pre-supermodel period, when her major rivals, according to Marie Claire's then-Fashion Director, Emma Bannister, were "Uptown Girl" star Christie Brinkley and "real American cheese" Carol Alt. So Iman stood out because she was striking, muscular, and African.'

Schermerhorn, as a third party, was able to hear everyone's grievances. 'I was near Hunt because no one else was. I was the go-between for everyone. They would come to me, all three of them, and tell me various things. I wanted to keep everything operating smoothly since I liked all of them.' 'The good news, and the bad news, was I was the guy who looked at the books every week with the tour manager and the office, keeping an eye on the money - so I was keeping the Sales brothers from renting limousines and the band from getting charged for David wanting a bigger hotel room because Iman was coming to visit, things like that,' Gabrels explained. On that tour, my sideburns actually turned gray in three months.'

David remained largely unaware of the band's internal squabbles. Only impending events in larger cities scared him - he was surprisingly apprehensive and performed better in smaller venues. Even after twenty-five years, he still paid too much attention to his press coverage, but he was unconcerned about the band's more strident critical slams: 'He realized it happened to everyone,' Gabrels says, 'that it cycles.'

It wasn't simply the critics who were disappointed. After promising early sales for Tin Machine's debut, sales had swiftly declined, with none of its singles making the Top 40. EMI balked at the thought of another Tin Machine record, so the band signed with Victory, a Polygram spinoff founded by Phil Carson, who had previously worked with Led Zeppelin at Atlantic. Tin Machine II offered some excellent tunes, such as Bowie and the Sales brothers' translucently gorgeous 'Goodbye Mr. Ed' and Gabrels' 'Shopping for Girls,' but, like the live dates, it didn't quite gel. The encounter was frustrating for Gabrels: 'I would have had one less Hunt Sales voice on the record,' he said, but David seemed unfazed. According to Eric Schermerhorn, playing and touring with Tin Machine allowed him to act like a "normal bloke." 'He'd be astounded by the most insignificant things. In Minneapolis, he walked into a pawn store with a lot of used radios and beat boxes and bought a used boombox for $65. "This is great!" he exclaimed. It seemed as though he'd never done that before.'

That occasional vulnerability alternated with trepidation in the autumn of 1991, owing primarily to his intention to propose to Iman. He proposed twice, both times in Paris, around the 29th of October: once on the Seine, to the strains of 'April in Paris,' and once at the Paris L'Olympia, where he reiterated his proposal on stage, in French, then played some saxophone as his admirers cheered. It may have been corny, but Schermerhorn admits, "but he was pretty amazing."

Just a few weeks later, in November 1992, Bowie found himself in Brixton, looking out the windows at Stansfield Road, crying, wondering how his life would have turned out if he'd become a shipping clerk or an accountant. Then, at David's childhood cinema, the Brixton Academy, Hunt Sales took over the mic for at least two songs too many, and a third of the audience fled before the finish.

Tin Machine's adventure had been exquisite, in a messed-up sense, but it was coming to an end. 'I recall him remarking to the whole band once at the rear of the bus, "Listen you guys, I'm getting older," recounts Schermerhorn. "I don't want to be doing this forever," David said. "I'd like to record one more song." He didn't want to play games.'

David remained publicly dedicated to Tin Machine; he stated at the start of the project that they would release three albums, and there was no evidence of his backing down. But back in Japan, he asked Schermerhorn what he was up to next and volunteered to make a few phone calls for him. Soon after, Schermerhorn would assist Iggy Pop in the creation of his final great album, 1994's American Caesar, which was inspired in part by David's recommendation that Iggy start reading history books. 'They were fantastic, contrasting characters. They'd each question me about the other. It's incredible: each wants what the other has. Perhaps Iggy was the better frontman. But David was a better boss because he wanted people to succeed after working with him. He wasn't required to assist me, yet he did.'

Reeves Gabrels was one of several persons who questioned the nature of fame during their time with David: it was considered as priceless, but its underlying value was impossible to measure. Reeves' conclusion was that it was 'a load of trash'; David, despite his contradictions, was glued to it. Even while he despised media intrusions, his fears necessitated that he court them, because his public persona - how he was regarded - was now an integral component of his own self-image. Thus, the most personal, agonizing emotions were something to be repressed as well as shown - most famously at the Freddie Mercury memorial concert on 20 April 1992, a few weeks after the Tin Machine tour ended.

The event was an odd combination, reflecting Queen's oddly diverse fan base, which ranged from heavy metallers like Guns N' Roses to Liz Taylor and Liza Minnelli. If Freddie wasn't a true personal buddy, their careers were closely interwoven, as two of the songs performed that night, 'All the Young Dudes' - a favorite of Brian May's - and 'Under Pressure' demonstrated. In a mint-green suit and Action Man hair, David looked composed and astonishingly well groomed next to Annie Lennox, who appeared to be made-up as Pris, the 'pleasure model' replicant from Bladerunner, and nuzzled provocatively against his cheek at the song's climax.

Only four days after the Wembley event, David married Iman in a secret civil ceremony in Montreux; once again, the public celebration at the American Church of St James in Florence highlighted David's dual desire for privacy and notoriety. The wedding was covered in a 23-page cover feature in Hello! magazine. David donned a white tie, while Iman wore a Herve Leger oyster gown with a train. Joey served as best man, Geoff MacCormack read Psalm 121, and Peggy posed for a portrait with Bono. Guests included Yoko Ono and Brian Eno. In the following interview, there were numerous moments of levity, as well as examples of history being rewritten: 'I don't think I ever really had what we could call a legitimate marriage,' he says of his time with Angie. There was a traditional, joyful air about him, as if he was relieved to finally put away his days of androgyny and defying moral standards and start again.

If the wedding was memorable, the album that commemorated it would be mostly forgotten, following Bowie's unfortunate recent trend of attempting and failing at commercial crossover. According to Reeves Gabrels, David was 'pressured' into hiring Nile Rodgers as producer for this upcoming project. Rodgers had overcome his animosity that, despite Let's Dance's massive success, David had rarely addressed its producer. He discovered, however, that he and Bowie had opposing goals for this new album from the start: 'I genuinely said to David, "David, let's kick Let's Dance in the ass," Rodgers adds. '"No, it's impossible," he responded. That is not something we can do." "What exactly do you mean we can't?" "I honestly don't know."

Taken on its own merits, as a snapshot of influences, Black Tie White Noise made sense, was endearing even, with its backstory of the wedding, the LA riots, and even, in 'Don't Let Me Down &

Down,' a song written by a Mauritanian princess and rendered both in the Indonesian language and a Brixton patois. The album was released with the usual fanfare, as well as a collective sigh of relief from the critical community that David had apparently ended his Tin Machine experimentation, as well as extensive promotion by David's new record company, Savage, an ambitious start-up business that paid a reported $3.4 million for the record in order to establish their credibility - a deal that ultimately ruined the company, which declared bankruptcy in December 1993 amid a flurry of lamentations.

Throughout the sessions, David was calm and amusing, with numerous flashes of his previous brilliance. When Nile was going to record his guitar solo for the twitchy, persistent 'Miracle Goodnight,' David gave him one of his signature, out-of-the-box orders. '"Imagine if the fifties never existed," he said. "Wow, now we're in some nebulous era," I thought, "because if the fifties hadn't happened, there would be no Jeff Beck and Hendrix." It was a fantastic direction.' Meanwhile, Gabrels provided the majority of his guitar work while Nile was filming The Tonight Show in California, working on numerous songs including 'You've Been Around' and a cover of Cream's 'I Feel Free' - a tune that David had recently revived with Tin Machine. Bowie later stated that he recorded the song as a tribute to Terry and the Cream event they had attended together at the Bromel Club; a second song, 'Jump They Say,' addressed his ex-brother more explicitly.

'I Feel Free' was enveloped in two layers of grief. Throughout the year, Bowie and the ailing Mick Ronson had regular communications; David had submitted numerous songs for the album Ronson was battling to finish, and had publicly praised Mick's production of Morrissey's Your Arsenal. Before Ronson arrived in the studio to contribute his unique sound, the new version of 'I Feel Free' was nearly finished; Gabrels' solo was eliminated to make room for his predecessor. 'It wasn't sad; it was just amazing to play with him and be around him,' explains Nile Rodgers. 'Mick simply did it, and it was cool,' says the author.

The album's sales were a powerful confirmation of Bowie's scorched-earth attitude with Tin Machine, and also seemed to show him fitting perfectly into the 1990s, while embracing his own past - influences like Mick and Terry - with a fresh honesty. Mick Ronson's death on April 30th marked the end of an era. However, the aftermath demonstrated that not all of David's demons had been exercised.

David offered a glowing tribute to his best-known lieutenant shortly after Ronson's death, saying, 'He was truly up there in the so-called hierarchy with the great guitar players... 'Outstanding, totally outstanding.'

There had been no official reconciliation following their divorce in their eighties because it was unnecessary - 'I've got no complaints, why would I?' Ronson told this reporter in 1989, but Bowie's relationship with the guitarist who had propelled him to prominence more than any other artist remained strained. The controversy erupted during Ronson's memorial concert at the Hammersmith Odeon the following April, where Bowie was noticeably missing.

'He had a couple of conflicts with some people on the bill and he didn't want to get involved,' said Trevor Bolder, Bowie's Spiders bassist and Ronson's long time buddy. Bolder also learned that David was concerned about performing in front of a small audience. 'All right. It's unfortunate that you have to be concerned about [such] things.' Others participating in the event, such as Suzi Fussey-Ronson, wonder, 'If he felt that the event wasn't big enough for him, why couldn't he have created a video to at least say something?'

When asked about it in 1998, Bowie said, 'The fact is I was not convinced by the intentions of this incident but, frankly, I prefer to stay silent.' Many of David's supporters questioned his reasons, particularly in light of his attendance at Freddie Mercury's memorial. Perhaps Bowie and Ronson's feud survived the guitarist's death. 'Another of Mick's singular abilities... was the ability to take a hook line that I might whistle or play badly and make it sing - we worked well together because of this talent of his as an interpreter,' Bowie says in his otherwise illuminating contributions to Mick Rock's book,

Moonage Daydream. Suzi Ronson was one of several who were insulted by Bowie's arrogant demeanor: 'Like David had prepared all his bloody solos. I spent $500 on that book and returned it because I was disappointed with it. After that, Mick Rock and I didn't communicate for a while.'

Ken Scott, the producer who witnessed their collaboration, agrees that there were times when David was very specific about some instrumental passages - '"Moonage Daydream" in particular' - but he disagrees with the suggestion that David humming Mick's solos to him was their standard practice. No. That's not how I recall it.' The icy relationship between the Bowie and Ronson camps was maintained by David's allusion in the same book to Suzi Fussey, Ronson's wife and David's long-serving personal assistant, as 'a local hairdresser in Bromley or Beckenham'. There were clearly portions of David's history with which he was not entirely at ease.

Bowie's late, ungracious remarks about Ronson were counterproductive: a case of The Dame doth protested too much, implying that David was more aware than he cared to accept how important Ronson was to his breakthrough. Certainly, the insignificant long-term impact of Black Tie White Noise - a pleasant, competent album that vanished from human consciousness along with the record company that released it - seemed to demonstrate David's reliance on a musical foil; a Ronson or a Brian Eno on whom he could feed, who made his music gel. He appeared to be trapped in a cycle of declining returns without one.

But that foil, that source of inspiration, didn't have to be a musician; in the case of David Bowie's best album in nearly a decade, a rushed commission done on a shoestring budget, the vital spark came from a relatively obscure novel about a Bromley childhood, which the BBC adapted into a film.

The idea for the project that would re-ignite Bowie's creativity came during a Q&A with one of David's favorite magazines, Interview, which was launched by Andy Warhol in 1969. As is customary, the magazine dispatched a famous figure to interview the month's cover star, and the choice of author Hanif Kureishi was especially astute:

the novelist, like David, was a Bromley lad and a fellow ex-student of Bromley Tech. In the final seconds of the interview, Kureishi said that the BBC was contemplating a TV adaptation of his 1990 novel, Buddha of Suburbia, which was inspired by Kureishi's own upbringing in south-east London. Kureishi jokingly inquired if David would contribute to the soundtrack. David agreed immediately. Just a few days later, the two were huddled over a mixing console at Mountain Studios.

The recording was divided into two sections: the first was a more traditional soundtrack written against a video of the shows, while the second was a more experimental soundtrack. Kureishi came in to watch, taken aback by the fact that his own work was being screened over a mixing desk 'dotted with dozens of buttons, levers, and swinging gauges', and later by the fact that David, noting a handful of pieces disrupted the tone of critical moments, swiftly rewrote them. The majority of the ideas utilized to accompany the drama were afterwards expanded into a full Bowie album. The hasty development of Buddha of Suburbia, like so many of Bowie's achievements, from The Idiot to 'Absolute Beginners,' aided its success. 'Something happened for that album,' Erdal Kizilcay explains. 'There wasn't a big budget, and David told us the tale before we started. It was a challenge, and the budget was limited, but David simply said, "Let's go, let's do it," and everything worked out.

Throughout the 1990s, several music writers recall that whenever a new David Bowie record was biked into the office, it was preceded by a publicist's assurance that 'it's his best since Scary Monsters.' The Buddha of Suburbia CD was a great evocation, not just of Kureishi's boyhood, but of his fellow Bromley lad, now aged forty-six, and was probably the only one sent across without such blandishments.

A few songs had been demoed, most notably the delicate yet anthemic 'Strangers When We Meet,' which David had attempted with Reeves during the Black Tie White Noise sessions, but the majority were assembled as first takes. They'd talk about a concept or a chord sequence, and Erdal'd remark, 'I'll try it.' 'Don't try it - play it!' David would exclaim. Erdal's personal journey was incorporated into the work, much of which was his improvisation - for example, the gloriously meandering 'South Horizon,' in which Kizilcay's simple trumpet motif, swinging drums, and busy bass duel with Mike Garson's piano, who'd just reappeared on the scene and overdubbed his part on the other side of the Atlantic.

'He is really a master - he knows exactly what he wants,' says David, referring to Erdal's musicianship. 'I was like his hands, his melodic hands,' he said. Even the more electro compositions, which were largely influenced by the newly formed Underworld, were rougher and more south London than White Tie's dance hits. 'The Mysteries' was sampled and reversed from an Austrian classical composition, similar to Low's 'Subterraneans'. The title tune, which cites Plaistow Grove, alongside the railway tracks; Terry, too, is mentioned by the words 'ouvre le chien,' a quote from David's 1970 song dedicated to his brother, 'All the Madmen'.

The album was released nearly unnoticed in the United Kingdom in November 1993 (it would take another two years for a US release on BMG), however the title tune reached number thirty-five in the UK singles chart. It was the best David Bowie album in a decade, and the first in twenty-two years to go completely unnoticed. Its inventor, the man who was usually focused on achievement, appeared not just unconcerned, but also very joyful,' according to his associate, Erdal Kizilcay.

Chapter 8: The Filthy Lesson of the Heart

By 1994, David seems to have devoted nearly as much energy changing himself into an underground artist as he did in transforming himself into a star. However, no one could have mistaken his way of living for that of a struggling musician. David and Iman spent most of their time in Los Angeles, Lausanne, and Mustique, where he kept an impeccably manicured home decorated in the airbrushed ethnic style of the most expensive international interior designers. Atop an old Indian mahogany lounger, he posed for Architectural Digest magazine. 'My objective,' he told writer William Buckley, 'is to make music so profoundly uncompromising that I have absolutely no audience left whatsoever - and then I'll be able to spend the entire year on the island.'

The comments reflected Bowie's sense of fun, yet there was a serious core to the sentiment. A run of good, arty ventures in the late 1990s, including a one-man display of twenty years' worth of paintings at a gallery on London's Cork Street in 1995 and a position on the editorial board of Modern Art magazine a year later, gave the impression that he was simply a wealthy hobbyist. But it wasn't true. In actuality, his need to be busy could not be suppressed indefinitely, and within months of this declaration, he was planning one of the most extreme recording experiences of his career - an art endeavor, but one he would fight to complete uncompromised.

The piece essentially harkened back to David's first trip to America, when he encountered the music of outsiders like Iggy Pop, the Legendary Stardust Cowboy, and the false Lou Reed. In January 1994, Bowie and Eno traveled to the Gugging Hospital outside Vienna, where psychiatrist Leo Navratil had assembled a group of patients who would become known as Outsider artists, hoping to tap a similar source in their quest to make the most extreme music of their careers. Navratil established a formal Haus der Künstler (house of artists) within the hospital in 1981, where these artists could live and work together as a community. 'Some of them don't even do [their art] as an expression of themselves; they do it because their work is theirs,' Bowie later told Interview magazine. Their motive for painting and sculpting is different from that of the normal artist who is sane in the eyes of society.'

Ingrid Sischy, the interviewer, was wise enough not to pursue the obvious question: whether David Bowie's half-brother might have benefited from a comparable progressive system rather than the dismal, understaffed confines of Cane Hill. Unsurprisingly, David and Eno were both tremendously moved by the experience of visiting the Haus der Künstler.

Reeves Gabrels arrived in Lausanne about a week before the record sessions to write and relax. In this new framework, he realized David might have eight hours set aside, six of which would be spent talking: 'but all of that informs the two hours when the flash hits'. The sessions were purposefully planned as an art happening. When David wasn't setting up their head space, chatting to them, and giving recommendations, he stood at an easel, sketching the band in charcoal. To reproduce the classic cut-up technique he'd employed on Diamond Dogs, he utilized a randomizing tool on his Apple Powerbook to create his lyrics. He was employing words for their sounds and connections, rather than a sequential narrative, as he had done in Berlin.

The path forward seemed obvious as they labored in Mountain's smoke-fogged studio, both Bowie and Gabrels chain-smoking one Marlboro after another. David had an easy artist to style himself after: Scott Walker, the man who had introduced him to Jacques Brel and whose career he had followed for the past twenty years, ever since hearing the singer in Lesley Duncan's room at Redington Road. 'Scott Walker was still one of David's heroes,' according to Gabrels, and the small group of musicians saw their project in a similar uncompromising vein to Scott's more challenging works.

But, as the album neared completion, David ran into the same difficulties as Scott Walker in finding a sympathetic record label. The brightest prospect, according to Gabrels, was Virgin America, now controlled by EMI; it was on their urging that David revised the record in January 1995, largely at the Hit Factory in New York. Carlos Alomar returns to add magnificent rhythm guitar to 'I Have

Not Been to Oxford Town'. Over the same period, they introduced another version of 'Strangers When We Meet', 'Thru These Architect's Eyes' and 'Hallo Spaceboy', which came from a Reeves' ambient track called 'Moondust'.

Bowie chose to lead with an uncompromising track - 'The Heart's Filthy Lesson' - accompanied by a purposefully inflammatory video produced by Sam Bayer, who was also responsible for Nirvana's 'Smells Like Teen Spirit'. The film was a gloriously squelchy snuff-movie assemblage, with a cabinet of freaks and sepia coloring reminiscent of Nine Inch Nails' 'Closer' video, which was notably shown on MTV with 'Scene Removed' signs to indicate the cuts. MTV refused to show Bowie's advertisement, which was ultimately broadcast in truncated form, and the single limped to number 92 in the US and number 35 in the UK.

The MTV youths with body piercings and tattoos building a Minotaur from spare body parts in Bayer's film captured the mid-nineties image so brilliantly that it suggested Bowie was simply riding on a fashionable bandwagon. He was the perfect person for the job. To be fair, groups such as Smashing Pumpkins, Marilyn Manson, Nine Inch Nails, and, of course, Nirvana, who recorded their clean version of 'Man Who Sold the World' in November 1993, all borrowed elements of Bowie's deep, claustrophobic sound. In any case, Bowie's foray into the MTV alternative scene was more about regaining his groove than it was about financial success.

Even when Bowie's music began to fade from young culture, he seemed to have a more thorough grasp of it as a father and forty-something. He projected a post-sexual society in 1971, putting together a youth manifesto that was, in retrospect, half-baked. Many of his statements regarding art elicited sniffles in the 1990s, with journalists like British writer Chris Roberts labeling him as "portentous." In retrospect, Roberts saw the significance of these seemingly little remarks. When the two met in 1995, Bowie anticipated a 'non-linear' society, telling him, "I think we as a culture embrace confusion." We're glad to recombine knowledge, and we move event horizons at breakneck speed. The generations - and I can use that plural now - beneath me can scan material far faster than my lot and don't necessarily look for the depth that we might.'

He'd summed up how the information society was changing in a few terms, forecasting how people would consume media in the next decades. However, there was an unmistakable implication within that reading that the cultural impact of a single pop singer, no matter how renowned, would be limited in the future years. The manifesto was growing less ambitious.

When Outside was being recorded, Bowie downplayed his fondness for younger bands like Nine Inch Nails, claiming that the Swiss industrialists The Young Gods were his main influences. When it came time to promote Outside on the road, however, Bowie chose to overtly identify himself with NIN frontman Trent Reznor, playing on a joint bill in a deliberately risky decision that exposed him to trend-hopping jibes and even hostile reactions.

Bowie's band now featured a new rhythm section of drummer Zachary Alford and bassist Gail Ann Dorsey, with George Simms on backing vocals, last seen on the Serious Moonlight tour; Peter Schwartz was chosen as musical director so David wouldn't have a 'favorite child' among Carlos, Reeves, or Garson: all previous incumbents. The tour began on September 14, 1995, in Hartford, Connecticut, and concluded in late October in Los Angeles. Bowie's 'Scary Monsters' and 'Subterraneans' were featured in Nine Inch Nails' performance, and he joined them for 'Reptile' and 'Hurt'.

David had gone through extensive psychological tactics with Brian Eno to overcome writer's block; for Earthling, just utilizing a computer performed the same thing. The tunes came quickly: words assembled on Post-It notes, judgments made on the fly, vocals recorded first or second take, with the exception of 'Little Wonder,' for which they ended up using the original guiding voice. Nearing his fifties, David's voice and writing sounded fresh, revitalized - there were many echoes of his youth, a Tony Newley inflection in 'Little Wonder,' or a trace of 'Letter to Hermione' in 'Dead Man Walking,' which also featured the simple two-note guitar riff Jimmy Page had shown him three decades earlier at IBC studios with The Manish Boys.

Earthling, on the other hand, did not keep the path if it came easily. Drum 'n' bass and Bowie's main preoccupation, Underworld, were both mainstream phenomenon by the time the album was released in January 1997; although many reviewers at the time applauded the revitalized lyricism, the album was doomed to be committed to history as another exercise in obvious bandwagon-jumping. The title, Earthling, sounded crassly self-referential, and the Alexander McQueen Union Jack frock coat appeared to be an attempt to cash in on the spring's buzzword, Britpop. Despite the appearance of dad at the disco, the fervor was genuine, and it spurred Bowie and Gabrels to sneak into events like that summer's Phoenix Festival, where they performed as the Tao Jones Index before their main show.

On January 8, 1997, David celebrated his fiftieth birthday at a packed Madison Square Garden, and the lineup looked meticulously arranged to highlight the birthday boy's cutting-edge credentials. Fans like the Smashing Pumpkins' Robert Smith, The Cure's Black Francis, and the Foo Fighters' Dave Grohl were there to duet on better-known songs, but his own set was dominated by material from his last two albums; Lou Reed - 'the King of New York,' as David aptly introduced him - was the only contemporary, joining him for 'Queen Bitch' and 'Waiting for the Man'. Only towards the end, after the crowd and band had sung him Happy Birthday, did he run through 'Under Pressure' and 'Heroes' and then finished the evening with a stunningly simple 'Space Oddity'.

It was a tremendous ceremony, a persuasive monument to his musical effect; however, while the show was being meticulously prepared, a more intimate package was being produced. Iman had been calling friends - some of whom hadn't seen David in years - for months, asking them to donate artwork to be bound into a book, each contribution noting a period in their lives with this purportedly cold, calculating character. According to those who have seen it, the piece, a compilation of drawings and prose, was wonderfully poignant, an unadorned tribute to a man who is simply, as boyhood buddy Geoff MacCormack puts it,'very humorous - a good mate'. Iman charmed each of her friends from Bromley, Berlin, and New York, uncovering new anecdotes about her husband. According to friends, only Iggy did not donate.

For many of David's friends, turning fifty was a watershed moment; for others, like Keith Richards, it was a chance to emulate heroes like John Lee Hooker and play late into the night. Iggy, who is only three months younger than David, used his fiftieth year on the earth to divorce his wife Suchi and go on a wild affair with an Argentinian female who inspired his crisis-ridden Avenue B album. David, on the other hand, appeared idyllically pleased with Iman, telling friends and even individuals he met casually - on a plane or in an airport shuttle - that getting married was the best thing that had ever happened to him: the absolutely traditional half of him seemed to have gained ascendancy.

Gabrels and Bowie had a musical relationship as close as any between Bowie and a fellow artist, made more complicated by the guitarist's younger generation, who had grown up listening to Bowie's music. Gabrels would vacillate between exhilaration at working with a childhood idol and annoyance at dealing with Bowie's business organization and niggles about percentage breakdowns on songwriting credits, which appeared to pop up around that time. Many of Bowie's musicians regard him as one of their best bosses - 'I'm his biggest fan, in that sense,' says Carlos Alomar - but others found working with Isolar consistently unpleasant. Bowie's management gave some partners, such as Erdal Kizilcay, the sense that he should take the offered proportion and consider himself lucky. The Bowie camp had a point - after all, any musician who worked with David was practically guaranteed an overnight transformation of their financial fortunes - but such arguments were especially difficult to swallow in the late 1990s, when David was gaining new fame, not for his music, but for the money he was rapidly amassing.

'Bowie Bonds,' the contentious method by which David raised $55 million in revenue from his back library, would cause a stir in the music industry. The bonds, which are securities issued against Bowie's future revenues over the next ten years, would also make

David Pullman a star. Pullman, the man most identified with the Bowie Bond, was awarded one of Time magazine's 100 Innovators at the age of thirty-nine, and went on to arrange similar deals for other performers. 'Linda's book gives readers a look at how exciting this industry can be,' gushed Pullman in a press release around the book's release in 2001.

Bowie reportedly received $55 million from the purchase (£39 million at 1997 sterling pricing), some of which was used to pay British taxes. David, on the other hand, desired the money for another reason: to repurchase his own songs.

When David originally split from Tony Defries in March 1975, he agreed to give Tony a portion of all the songs David recorded up until 1982. This was a sliding scale - supposedly a whole 50% of Bowie's share on pre-1975 albums, and less after that - but the money was due in perpetuity. Defries kept co-ownership of the masters, and even claimed the right to release additional Bowie recordings; a privilege he used beginning in the early 1990s, with the publication of the Santa Monica 72 live album in 1994, as well as subsequent albums based on BBC and Astronettes sessions. By the mid-1990s, Isolar had begun negotiations with their predecessor to purchase out Bowie's rights. According to Defries' acquaintances, the conversations were cordial: David's representatives told Defries' representatives that he wanted the assets "to pass on to his children." None of the parties involved have ever confirmed how much of David's $55 million went to Defries, but some speculate it was at least half. If that's the case, Tony Defries made nearly $27 million, an outstanding return on the £500,000 he paid Laurence Myers for Bowie's masters in the summer of 1972.

Over the years, the idea of Bowie Bonds came up again and again, sometimes with the implication that David, like Mick Jagger, was preoccupied with money: a lower-middle-class youngster trying to compensate for childhood austerity. Few people noticed that, at the age of fifty, he was paying tens of millions of dollars to regain his own life's work. Following the acquisition, Tony Defries purchased an outstanding home in Virginia and now had tens of millions of dollars to invest, a profession in which he had always excelled. David had bought his own past.

If the reasons for Bowie's request for extra $55 million were misinterpreted, the uproar signaled a time when his name was inextricably linked with capitalism. The implications of the Bowie Bonds were closely watched within the financial world, yet a series of lawsuits between Pullman and various other parties contending over who originated the bonds took the shine off them. The ultimate judgment revealed that the bonds were inspired not by financial wizard David Pullman, but by David's own business manager, Bill Zysblat. The debate over the matter would never die away. Lamont Dozier, the famed Motown songwriter, would subsequently sue the consultants who worked on his own bond offering; in the aftermath of EMI's financial woes, Moody's, the major credit ratings agency, lowered Bowie Bonds to one notch above junk grade in 2004.

David had become as obsessed with the internet as he had with art and music in recent years: 'He was right at the forefront, and it made sense he would be,' says Thomas Dolby, Bowie's Live Aid piano player. Dolby had relocated to the West Coast of the United States to begin an online start-up, and Bowie had shared his excitement with him. 'It was a hedonistic thing, living in the present, getting a kick out of what he was experiencing.' Dolby had witnessed peers like David Byrne graduate from hanging out at the Mudd Club to investigating the medium of video. 'These were the creative lightning rods. And he was ecstatic because he saw a return to a grass-roots movement. He could have a ringside seat and be in command, do things on the spur of the moment, and receive immediate response.'

Bowie's life would be documented online for at least the next decade, but his influence extended beyond his own website and music. According to several industry insiders, he was planning the future of the internet. Later, technology writer John Naughton referred to Bowie as a "leading futurologist," having made some of the "most perceptive observations anyone has ever made about our networked world." Bowie understood the web's potential for creating new communities in the late 1990s, but he also saw the long-term ramifications for copyright, predicting how creativity and intellectual property would be jeopardized. In 2002, he predicted that music would "become like running water or electricity," foreshadowing the emergence of streaming services like Spotify. Bowie would never describe himself as a visionary, and his thoughts on the evolution of modern culture were mainly limited to promotional interviews. However, his foresight spurred Naughton to say in 2010, 'If you want to foresee the future, ask a musician.'

By January 1998, David began pushing the introduction of his own websites, davidbowie.com and bowieart.com, as well as the debut of BowieNet (membership price $19.95 per month) on September 1, 1998. Outside, his public relations firm, recalls the launch as 'one of the most stressful things I can remember, there would be webcasts with him, Boy George, Visconti - and he just enjoyed it'. David's passion - he'd also drop in on his own chat rooms, using the handle sailor' - was partly recreational; he'd spend hours surfing the internet or shopping for bargains on eBay.

The Bowie brand was established online in the same year that the man himself was introduced as an independent digital entity. David summoned Reeves Gabrels to London near the end of 1998 to accompany him and Iman to a meeting with the computer game developer Eidos. The creator required more than just a soundtrack; 'They wanted David, Iman, and me to be characters in a game,' Gabrels explains. 'So we began discussing how to accomplish it, set up in a hotel room, and began writing.' The resulting game, Omikron, was a cult classic, albeit not a mainstream success, but 'Survive,' the main song Bowie and Gabrels wrote for the game, was a gem, simple and unaffected, almost Scary Monsters in vibe, without any of the over-complexity and over-thinking that seemed synonymous with Bowie in the 1990s.

It was perhaps natural that a meeting that would have a tremendous effect on his future work occurred as a result of a children's cartoon during that most multimedia of years. David had been requested to contribute a song to the Rugrats movie (also featuring Iggy), and summoned Tony Visconti to produce the oddly retro song, 'Safe'. Visconti's eyes 'welled up' as he answered the phone. I had forgotten how much I missed him.' Unfortunately, the song did not make it into the film since the sequence in which it was included was edited. But their romance had been revived.

Most listeners saw Bowie's fall mood as him reflecting on his life. 'It was autobiographical, but it wasn't his biography, it was someone close to him,' David told Reeves. There was some debate about whether he was writing from my perspective. I'm not sure. The end was approaching. I knew I had to depart; it simply took me a while to figure out how.'

Gabrels had helped Bowie escape the creative rut of the late 1980s, but both sides felt it was time to move on. Mark Plati, Earthling's computer genius, had now taken on a more traditional role as bassist, a transition mostly prompted by Reeves. As a result, Gabrels had prepared his own substitute. 'I was literally burning out,' says the guitarist, explaining why there was no falling out. Much of it had less to do with David and more to do with time away from home, time on the road, and dealing with some of the people around him. 'I thought it was friendly.'

Of all the regrets David ever expressed in public, the fact that his son had such an unusual upbringing was the one he addressed the most. Joey had worked briefly with handicapped children in Switzerland and at the Jim Henson puppet studio - a connection he'd made during his father's work on Labyrinth - after leaving Gordonstoun, before receiving a scholarship to the College of Wooster in Ohio to study Philosophy. He began using his given first name, Duncan, once he arrived. In 1999, David suggested Duncan accompany him on the set of Tony Scott's television series The Hunger; Scott became Duncan's mentor, initiating a love affair with movies. The 'calm and pleasant' Duncan enrolled at Covent Garden's International Film School in February 2000, according to the Daily Mail.

David knew there would be parallels with the summer Duncan was born since Glastonbury organizer Michael Eavis had called him before Christmas, urging him to return to the event, twenty-nine years after his first visit. Earl Slick returned to the fold in the spring, joining Plati, Gail Ann Dorsey, drummer Sterling Campbell, and backing singers Holly Palmer and Emm Grynner. Three warm-up events were scheduled in New York, one of which was canceled due to his voice failing. Perhaps it was for this reason that David was visibly apprehensive before his Sunday night slot at the event on June 25.

David was still referring to his main work as 'daddyfying' a year after Alexandria was born, his delight at the new experience as all-consuming as his childhood obsessions. There was a short interlude filming a humorous, self-parody cameo for Ben Stiller's film Zoolander, plus additional frustrating weeks fighting with complications over the completed Toy album - in June David mentioned scheduling conflicts with EMI/Virgin. In truth, this was a final spat caused by managerial disagreements within the corporation. As far as anyone could tell, he seemed indifferent about the inconveniences and had adjusted into life in New York. The public saw him as a culture buff, always going to the ballet or a new exhibition, or hanging out with local musicians like Moby or Lou Reed, which he did. But he was equally content Googling at random in 'the bunker,' his computer and work room, waking up at 6 a.m. and dealing with emails before taking Lexi for a stroll around SoHo or Greenwich Village in her buggy, or sitting chatting with Iman over a bowl of pasta by a restaurant window, the two of them smiling graciously if they were interrupted by a fan.

David's belief that, as a new father, he was coming to terms with his own past grew stronger in the aftermath of his mother's death. Margaret Mary Jones' death was reported on April 2nd, and it had come 'out of the blue' for David. Several familiar characters from his upbringing attended the funeral, including Ken Pitt and Pat Antoniou, the aunt who had publicly accused David of being insensitive to his half-brother, extending the feuds that had dogged the Burns family for half a century. When David spotted her, he "walked straight over, threw his arms around her," says Ken Pitt, the only man who had kept in touch with all of the family's many branches. 'He was simply fantastic.'

Others would remain after a spirit was placed to rest. Freddie Buretti died of cancer on May 11 in Paris. Almost all of the costumes Freddie had fashioned for him had been saved by David. And the problems with Toy grew worse over the summer, with the record becoming a casualty of Mariah Carey's legendarily disastrous album, Glitter, which sold so poorly that Virgin was forced to pay a reported $19 million to terminate her contract early; Nancy Berry, who had signed both Bowie and Carey, was fired. But, even before the album's demise, David was already arranging its replacement. In June, he visited Tony Visconti and his new girlfriend in their 'humble', drafty, three-story wooden apartment in West Nyack, New York. They worked on tunes together at Tony's loft, just as they did in the Haddon Hall basement, except this time they copied and pasted ideas using Pro Tools software instead of Mark Pritchett's Revox. Tony took David to Allaire, a gorgeous wood-lined recording studio nestled in the Catskill Mountains: it seemed like a wonderfully made Edwardian boat, with panoramic views over the reservoir that quenches New York City, on their second day. 'I knew exactly what lyrics I was going to compose the instant I walked into the studio,' David later explained, 'even if I didn't yet know what the words themselves were.'

When they began recording, David brought his "little family," who resided in a tiny house on the grounds portion of the time, and stayed there until the album was essentially finished. He got up around five o'clock one morning, as was his custom, glanced out the windows, and noticed two deer feeding beneath the field in the early morning light. A car drove slowly past the reservoir in the distance, and suddenly words began to flow from him, as tears streamed down his face. 'Heathen' was the song: 'I didn't like writing it. It had a foreboding and final feel to it.' The lines read as though he is saying goodbye to a lover, yet the thing he is addressing is life.

For the past two decades, Bowie had struggled with the question of whether he could ever 'give so aggressively' again in his latter years. He had found his answer in the peaceful, almost mystical atmosphere of Allaire, as a revitalized confidence and passion pervades each of the songs. Where Hunky Dory speaks of rebirth, of the shiny and new, Heathen displays a hard-won confidence in a life well lived, like beautifully worn leather - the quirky, almost baby voice on 'A Better Future'; drifting, dark, drum loops on 'The Angels Have Gone'; impassioned singing, reminiscent of 'Heroes', on 'Slow Burn'.

There wasn't the visceral pleasure of Bowie in his twenties and thirties, but there was a sense that this was a legendary album, one that didn't pale in contrast to Scary Monsters.

Many of the album's reviews were influenced by the fact that Bowie and Visconti were still in the Catskills on 9/11; David was on the phone with Iman, who was back in the flat, as the second jet hit. When David returned to Manhattan, there was an alarming gap in the kitchen window's familiar vista; Iman realized that many of the men who used to greet her and Lexi as she rolled the buggy by the local Fire Department station a couple of streets away were probably dead. It would solidify the family's affinity with the city; David would lead the Concert for New York in October and would stop talking about relocating back to London. But, despite the fear and uncertainty in the air, David was infectiously positive, retelling Lexi's baby words verbatim to friends, reading her books, and assuring people around him how lucky he was.

The Heathen tour ended in late October 2002, with shows in each of New York's five boroughs, but David was already planning new songs as he returned to his daily routine of walks and reading sessions with Lexi, visits to Iman at her cosmetics company's 7th Avenue office, or his three-times-a-week boxing sessions at a nearby gym.

After a few days of pre-production in November, he and Visconti were ready to resume production in January. This time, they recorded in New York, at Looking Glass, but in a smaller studio, which resulted in a more confined, urban vibe 'to express the anxiety of NYC,' according to Visconti. He and David collaborated closely, making quick decisions; the recording was straightforward, with much of it done with David's touring band. Mike Garson, like Chuck Hammer and Dominic Muldowney before him, was impressed by how intuitive their musical relationship was: "I worked with Tony Visconti with perfect love." He's a fantastic man.'

David had developed an unrivaled ability for eliciting the best from musicians throughout his life; in only two songs, 'The Loneliest Guy' and 'Bring Me the Disco King,' he seemed to reach through Garson to spark something fresh. The last track, with Garson's sparse, milky chords supported by a Heathen drum loop, was as good as anything they'd done together in the previous thirty years. 'You promised me the finish would be clear,' David said, his voice clouded by four decades of Gitanes and Marlboros; after twenty-eight albums, he was still composing songs that were fiercely subdued yet revealed new secrets with repeated listens.

From The Spiders on, one of the most common criticisms leveled against David's work was that he exploited his musicians and influences - that he was more of a curator than a creative. However, as Garson attests, he possessed a practiced, effective, and almost mystical capacity to inspire them to create something wholly new: 'Somehow his beingness and essence bring out the best in people,' adds the pianist. 'He could give you minor guidance but never says do this or do that. I always tend to play my best things in his space, to contribute every facet of my playing. I don't think I would have thought of those solos if he hadn't been present.'

Garson, in his own manner, summarizes all of the challenges surrounding how David elicited music from his bandmates. In his early days, the term 'vampiric' was used several times to describe how he benefited from the inventiveness of other musicians. Yet, as Garson points out, he rarely took from them; rather, he inspired them to generate concepts that would not have existed without him. In these years, David Bowie was always modest about the achievements to which he laid claim; but he was demonstrably correct when he told Livewire.com: 'To not be modest about it, you'll find that with only a couple of exceptions, most of the musicians that I've worked with have done their best work by far with me. I can highlight their own strengths. 'Take them somewhere they would never have gone on their own.' This was a daring allegation, but it was true, as Garson and others attested. He did not accept. He contributed.

When Tony Visconti next met David, he thought he looked fatigued. Reality was released on September 15, 2003, to positive reviews, and by October, David had begun his biggest tour in five years. In retrospect, the signs had been building for months, but the tour was exciting at the time: 'We didn't rest on our laurels - at one point, we had sixty or seventy songs in our repertoire,' explains Garson. 'He'd call things out of nowhere occasionally, and we'd simply play them in front of 3,000 people. It was quite daring.' However, on November 12th, the Toulouse show was canceled due to David contracting laryngitis; two days later, they proceeded, only for the first leg of the US tour to be postponed by a week due to David contracting influenza. In January, he was back on the road, but tragedy struck on May 6, 2004, in Miami, when the night's concert was canceled due to the death of a lighting engineer. Then, on June 18, his outdoor gig in Oslo was cut short when a female fan threw a lollipop into the socket of his left eye. For a few moments, his composure wavered as he demanded to know who had thrown the object; then, relaxing, he reminded them, 'I've only got one good eye, you know,' before assuring them he meant revenge by extending the concert. Five nights later, in Prague, David pulled his concert short after fifteen songs due to what seemed like a trapped nerve in his shoulder. On Saturday, June 25, he performed one final act at the Hurricane Festival in Scheessel, Germany, before fainting backstage in agony.

For the next nine days, BowieNet would broadcast a message stating that the tour had been canceled "due to ongoing pain and discomfort from a trapped/pinched nerve." Only when David returned to New York on July 8 did his publicist reveal that he had emergency angioplasty surgery for a blocked artery. Two days later, press reports claimed a tour insider as saying David had a heart attack backstage and had surgery the night of his collapse: 'The heart surgery wasn't routine. It was far more serious than anyone is admitting.' David's friends would later learn that the procedure involved stents, which are spring-like mesh tubes fitted inside an artery to keep it open - a less invasive alternative to heart bypass surgery, which happened to be a specialty of the Klinik St Georg in Hamburg, where he was rushed following the Scheessel show.

David was caught roaming around the streets of New York City's Chinatown on July 28. He shook hands with well-wishers while wearing a stetson and a green T-shirt, then entered a health food store to load up on tea and a range of ancient Chinese treatments. Iman informed friends a year later that David was still composing and recording: 'We're not retiring folks,' she claimed.

Chapter 9: Houdini's Mechanism

Fans continued to think that aliens are immortal in the months following David's heart attack, punctuated by tantalizing glimpses of the man in the audience for gigs by Gail Ann Dorsey, Arcade Fire, and the rare red-carpet event. David returned to the spotlight more than a year later, on September 8, 2005, in an evening packed with nerves, emotion, and affection.

The rehearsal for the Condé Nast Fashion Rocks benefit for Hurricane Katrina victims was nerve-racking. Bowie hadn't met his single accompanist, Mike Garson, until their rehearsal the afternoon before the concert. Various performers and staff were working around Radio City Music Hall as they ran through the tune. 'Everyone who was performing that night was listening - you could hear a pin drop,' Garson realized as he rippled into the opening chords at the practice. 'Life on Mars?,' the song given to the twenty-three-year-old Bowie on the bus to Lewisham, sounded completely different from any prior rendition.

David was even more hesitant; he was out of practice, even scared: 'You have a heart disease, you've got to be wondering, "Am I going to drop dead on stage?"' recalls Garson. 'Anything may go through your mind - you've been through a hard patch, and you don't know if it'll happen again.' Yet, for Garson, there was something beautiful about the moment as Bowie relaxed slowly into the song in front of an excited audience: the fact that their interpretation was on the edge and vulnerable gave it a new depth. 'It was heartfelt and sentimental. It was extraordinary - one of the most profound things we've ever done, with elements that transcend musical laws such as rhythm, harmony, melody, and intonation. It was something more profound. It was almost heavenly in nature.'

The sight of David stepping up to the mike-stand, nervously grasping it almost as if for comfort, was moving and - as the camera panned to reveal him wearing high-water pants, bare ankles, a bandaged wrist, and a black eye - slightly comical. With David's pitch lowered by half an octave, there was a sensation of the seasons shifting from spring to fall. The song was first performed by a young buck as a snide challenge to Sinatra. Even at a lower key, the wonderful octave jump to 'Mars' that had launched a career was no longer simple and transcendent; it spoke of pain. David Bowie was not confronting the Chairman of the Board; rather, he was following in his footsteps. 'He came out that night as a mature vocalist, like Tony Bennett or Frank Sinatra: someone with presence. A gentleman in his fifties who would never attempt to accomplish anything that a twenty-year-old would. 'It was incredible,' adds Garson.

David Bowie, an older gentleman, was a sight that his followers found difficult to bear. As still photos and then videos - the kind of view behind the gilded curtain that would have been unthinkable in the MainMan era - spread around the world wide web, where Bowie fans lived, reactions ranged from affection and sympathy to horror and ridicule: 'He's a mess,' was one of the kinder opinions. 'He seems a bit ... dead,' states YouTube commentator Lindadox, before adding insult to injury: '[and] the hair isn't exactly working for him'.

David's virtual appearances were also becoming less regular. Since 2005, David Bowie's postings in his BowieNet blog had been more sporadic, until on 5 October 2006, he published the most exuberant article in years: 'Yesterday I got to be a character on - tan-tara - SpongeBob SquarePants. We are overjoyed as a family. Nothing else needs to happen this year, or at least not this week.' Nothing else worked. For in January 2007, it was announced that a scheduled live date, which was supposed to close a Bowie-curated Highline festival the following May, had been secretly canceled. Instead of the Bowie show, there was a live rendition of 'The Fat Little Man' with Ricky Gervais, followed by... nothing.

Given David Bowie's incredible work pace over the preceding forty years, the notion that this was the calm before a new surge of activity was logical as he disappeared from the music world. The off-the-cuff comment, 'simply don't participate,' signified a fleeting dissatisfaction. The notion of permanent retirement sounded inconceivable - except that it was something David had wished for for at least twenty years.

'He does always appear pretty vibed up,' says director Julien Temple, referring to Bowie's desire for an escape during the pause after Tonight. But perhaps he isn't underneath.'

Temple had accompanied the artist to Brixton Carnival during that time, watching his minders make a route ahead of him and witnessing the problems of "that bubble life." While watching David work in three different eras of his career, the director noticed that the most difficult challenge David faced was the "grueling nature of reinvention." The massive creative surge required to achieve that repeatedly. It has a psychological cost that goes beyond the usual clichés of celebrity. The strains of celebrity do take their toll, even on David, who may not appear to be as affected as others.'

During their conversations in 1987 and 1989, Bowie expressed a wish to 'escape: to parachute out, to develop a method that would deliver a beautiful departure' to Temple. Of course, Bowie's career was spiraling downward creatively throughout those years. The response of Never Let Me Down, as well as the failure of Glass Spider, had pushed back Bowie's dream of releasing 'a real, dazzling escape mechanism - a kind of Houdini escape from pop stardom.'

For well over a decade, at least a part of David Bowie had been hoping for that great exit, that one grandiose explosion behind which he could vanish. Finally, mortality gave its own less spectacular escape route. And, as one of David's pals puts it, "If you were in the hospital after a heart attack, would you wish you'd spent more time flogging yourself on tour?" Or would you want to spend more time with your five-year-old?'

Meanwhile, many around David had moved on. Coco has returned from California and is once again working closely with David. She has spent decades of her life caring for him, and her responsibilities are now less burdensome. She now has time to go on walks throughout Manhattan, accompanied by her dog.

Iggy Pop reconnected with his Stooges, who were feted at festivals throughout the world, but by the late 1990s, David had lost touch with the guy who had profited the most from his assistance. When journalist Robert Phoenix inquired about their friendship, David admitted, 'I probably shouldn't talk about it,' while adding, 'We have drifted apart from each other.' The issue was a basic clash of egos: 'Jimmy had come to detest the fact that he couldn't do a fucking story without my name being referenced,' he explained. Iggy has just restored his connections with former Stooges guitarists Ron Asheton and James Williamson, with whom he had a dramatic falling out. When he talks about David, a man he was undeniably closer to, he retains some reserve. 'I suppose in every close friendship you may use the word "love" - and in many friendships you'll notice that one person loves the other more than the other loves him or her,' says a mutual friend of the two. David, I believe, loved Jim more than Jim loved David. And, in the end, I believe Jim discovered he could function without him.' Iggy, who is three months younger than David, is still touring with the reunited Stooges. In person, he appears fragile, with a perceptible limp, but he enters the stage with the exuberant enthusiasm of a spring lamb.

More ramifications of Bowie and MainMan's tumultuous relationship rumbled on: in 2009, five years after Bowie Bonds were downgraded to one notch above junk grade by credit rating agency Moody's, headlines throughout the world read, 'Is Bowie to blame for the credit crunch?' The worldwide financial catastrophe, according to BBC writer Evan Davis, was caused by bankers who drew their inspiration from David Bowie; seeing him securitize his future income, they followed his lead with their mortgage company, with devastating repercussions. (Subsequently, more financial experts chimed in to mock the claim.) Bowie's personal finances are reported to have decreased gradually during the recession; in 1997, Business Age magazine placed his wealth at $917 million, however this is widely viewed as an exaggeration by most financial experts; a recent Sunday Times poll estimated his value at £100 million. Outside of EMI, his back library will be available for licensing again in 2012, and many fans are hoping to see more of what is regarded to be the most intriguing collection of unreleased audio and video outtakes of any major recording artist.

Duncan's interviews provided a revealing glimpse into David Bowie's father's life: there were stories about how they'd worked on stop-frame animation together, and about David bringing home his illicit Star Wars DVDs. There was also indication that David had kept a respectful distance in order not to overshadow his son. (Bill Zysblat, David's business manager, was recognized as executive producer on the picture, but Mr Jones senior was not mentioned.) 'I think we always loved each other, but he was traveling and working a lot, and I was in his custody, so it was... tricky, because obviously there were people who would look after me, but a lot of the time he might not be around,' Duncan says of his upbringing. As a result, it was an unconventional relationship.'

David had frequently expressed his guilt over his son's turbulent childhood, but the overwhelming positive response to Moon, which was made for the unthinkably small budget of $5 million, grossed $6 million in the first nine weeks of release, and picked up two international awards before finally clinching Duncan a BAFTA award for Most Promising Newcomer in February 2010. Jones gently denied that his tiny science-fiction gem was influenced by his father's 'Space Oddity' (or even Kubrick's 2001), instead mentioning later influences like Silent Running and Bladerunner. But there was a lot of parallel with his father's work. The solitude and loneliness of the only protagonist, Sam Bell, reflect Duncan Jones' lonely childhood and his father's isolation. More profoundly, Bell finds solace in sculpting a church out of balsa wood: an image that echoed Merrick's cardboard church, or the 'cathedral made of matchsticks' that David had lauded in one of his Heathen interviews as a symbol of the British amateur tradition - that compulsion to perfect a job, whether or not anyone will see it. Finally, Bell is imprisoned in a cycle of reincarnation, wearing out each new manifestation of himself until, like Bowie, he achieves his 'Houdini escape'.

David's unexpected appearance with Duncan at the Sundance Film Festival on January 23, 2009, was a short but brilliantly timed occasion; remaining in front of the camera long enough to create a rush of press for the film, David, dressed in gray, let his son do the talking. Duncan praised his father for giving him 'the time to sort out what I wanted to accomplish - since it's taken me a while' during a Q&A following the screening.

This would be Bowie's only media appearance of the year, along with an appearance alongside Iman for Moon's premiere at New York's Tribeca Film Festival in April; by 2010, Iman would generally appear on red carpets solo, until David turned up in a tux and black scarf for his wife's acceptance of her 'Fashion Icon' award. Every few months, a new reissue would appear: a DVD based on his VH1 Storytellers appearance, ten years after it was recorded; a fortieth-anniversary edition of the Space Oddity album, complete with an iPhone app allowing fans to mix their own version of David's debut hit; and, later, the announcement of an illustrated book of Bowie artifacts.

For many, Bowie's continued absence appeared like an awful betrayal. Fewer and fewer of them are paying the $60-per-year subscription price to BowieNet, and the bowie art website was shut down permanently in 2008. The faithful congregate on the internet, their numbers dwindling. Despite the ongoing reissues of his classic works, there is a growing consensus among fans and business figures that this man is not preserving his work; that it is like a grand mansion with weeds blooming in the garden and paint chipping from the window frames. What could he be doing that was more essential than looking after them?

David, his old friend, would eventually bring him the success he desired. George developed himself as an artist and illustrator during the same time period, creating scores of record and book covers for David, Marc Bolan, and numerous others. Today, sitting in his lovely, airy north London home, his artworks adorning the walls like gems, there is still a sense of awe at what his friend accomplished. Not for the money or the glory, but for the simple question, 'Wasn't he brave? to act like he did?'

With the adoration comes a sense of what David missed out on: family life, all the little tokens of which surround us, images, well-worn artifacts that suggest a well-worn life. I feel sorry for Underwood's friend for a second. Then George emphasizes how

David has lived his life "backwards." How the twenty-year-old who adored children is now, at the age of sixty, able to spend time with his own. A few weeks later, I run into some old acquaintances whom David has reconnected with, telling them about his nine-year-old daughter, as if what she's up to is more intriguing than his present career. He'll frequently start a phone call by connecting with Lexi. As if there was a legacy more essential than the hundreds of songs known to be in Bowie's vault.

Similar epiphanies have occurred in subsequent generations. Bowie has been chastised for referring to himself as a cult artist, a seemingly absurd remark for someone with so many Top 10 hits, yet there is truth in this, because his music continues to speak to outsiders, those who are either on the edge or want to be. Bowie of Low, "Heroes," and The Idiot called to Black Francis of the Pixies, whose music would define the so-called alternative rock era of the 1990s: "It was so brave." This sentiment is repeated: 'He exhibited no fear,' adds Nicolas Godin of Air, who found the same trio of records while studying architecture in Versailles. 'He's the entire artist - the look, the voice, the capacity to write, the stage presence,' Godin says of Bowie's influence on the French band's 'modest' career. The splendor. Nobody is like that these days. Everyone can be reached; he was inaccessible.'

John Lennon, who acted as David Bowie's elder brother, occasionally lamented that the world expected more from his band. He'd tell people, 'What more could you want?' after the Beatles had released eleven albums together. David Bowie is allowed to share Lennon's sentiment as he meanders around New York, watching his daughter grow up. Even those who have worked with David in the past can't help but share the fans' hope that this man will once again unleash the music that is otherwise trapped within. 'I'm waiting,' Mike Garson, his longest-serving pianist, says. 'There is no magic in the air right now. We're in a rut, so maybe in a couple of years he'll start hearing the next thing.

Even still, the enigmatic alchemy remains a mystery. Can the man who reinvented himself ever do it again?

'Who knows if he's not experiencing it,' Garson says. 'An artist knows when to take a break. Why do anything if you don't feel or hear it? 'We'll see what happens.'

Printed in Great Britain
by Amazon